THE POWER OF
PERCEPTION

THE POWER OF PERCEPTION

Eliminating Boundaries to Create Successful Global Leaders

**DIANE HAMILTON, PH.D.
AND MAJA ZELIHIC, PH.D**

Paradise Valley, Arizona

*The Power of Perception: Eliminating Boundaries
to Create Successful Global Leaders*

Published by DIMA Innovations, LLC
Paradise Valley, Arizona

ISBN (hardcover): 9781642379693
ISBN (paperback): 9781642379709
eISBN: 9781642379716

Testimonials

A profound piece of work from Dr. Diane Hamilton and Dr. Maja Zelihic. They wrote, "perception is reality in the workplace." What I really appreciate about this book is that they clearly see the potential to change the reality of the workplace by thoughtfully changing one's perception of that reality –a powerful, paradigm-changing thought. Well done, Diane and Maja!

Doug Conant

Founder & CEO, Conant Leadership; Chairman, The CEO Force for Good; Former CEO, Campbell Soup; Former Chairman, Avon Products

Perception is such a powerful force in our everyday lives, but few of us really understand how it works, how it affects us, and how we can better use it to our advantage. Drs. Hamilton and Zelihic have written a definitive, practical, and actionable guide to comprehending the power of perception and harnessing it with intention.

Jeff Hoffman

Chairman of the Board at Global Entrepreneurship Network, Hollywood film producer, Grammy and Emmy-Award Winner Producer

It is extremely rare to find a book that can change your life, and this is one of them. The Power of Perception gives you tools and ideas that will shift the way you look at the world and dramatically increase both your personal and leadership success.

John Spence

Global Business Expert, Former CEO of an International Rockefeller Foundation

Perceptions define our existence. How great to see a book that not only acknowledges this fact but also offers the hope of improving our world by seeing things differently.

Jim McKelvey

Co-founder of Square and Author of The Innovation Stack: Building an Unbeatable Business one Crazy Idea at a Time.

Recognizing the value of perception is critical to an organization's success. Drs. Diane Hamilton and Maja Zelihic examine the importance of perception and how it can empower people to feel like they contribute in distinct ways. This recognition can lead to a clear ROI, with more productive employees who have fewer conflicts.

Laura Huang

Associate Professor at Harvard Business School; Author of Edge: Turning Adversity into Advantage

Perception is everything, it is the way we see the world, the canvas we behold. Drs. Hamilton and Zelihic's book makes the concept of Perception so very reachable for all. It brings to the forefront the power that perception can create in our lives and what we can do to harness this as a powerful tool. A must read for anyone interested in creating greater success and thus a more profound life.

Rhiannon Reese

Top 10 Global Coach, CEO of The Conscious Coaching Collective, Author of How to Climb Mount Everest in Sandals

Understanding how to manage that is an increasingly important issue in a globalizing world where diversity is paramount to success, making this book a must read.

Bethany McLean

Journalist, Author of The Smartest Guys in the Room: The Amazing Rise and Scandalous Fall of Enron

Dedication

For G. Ross Kelly, without whom this book would not be possible. His perception of the meaning of our lives, our abilities, and the positivity that we should have when faced with challenges, continues to inspire us.

Table of Contents

Foreword

Whether leaders of companies strive to increase distribution, analyze retailing opportunities, market, source manufacturing, or a hundred other activities, they must consider the varied impact of perception. In today's competitive landscape, leaders often look to me for advice and expertise to navigate a continually changing environment. We live in a time where diversity is critical for success. Yet, we must navigate successfully to avoid conflict.

Some of the best advice I received came from guidance from mentorship from my father and other great minds, including Zig Ziglar, who famously said, "You will get all you want in life if you help enough other people get what they want." But how do you know what they want? Should it be based on your perception or theirs? If it is based on theirs, how do you discover what that is? The starting point is to be inquisitive.

In Mentor to Millions, my co-author Mark Timm, and I wrote about the value of curiosity. By asking questions, we can learn more about other people's perceptions and preferences in life.

Authors Dr. Diane Hamilton and Dr. Maja Zelihic have tapped into the critical process involved in perception. What might seem perfectly reasonable or acceptable to one person might be entirely unacceptable for another; recognizing how our IQ, emotional intelligence, culture, critical thinking, and curiosity impact our reality is an essential part of being successful in business.

Having heard more pitches than I can count, I can tell you that getting an outside perception of a situation can be the key to success. The sage leader relies on more than their perception. They recognize that it is fundamental to meet people's needs based on their customers' and employees' expectations and vision. Now is the time to focus on pivoting, which includes recognizing the impact of how we, and others, view reality in our business and personal lives. It is through our empathy that we gain from that process that we can be truly successful.

Kevin Harrington

Kevin Harrington is the Inventor of the Infomercial, an Original Shark on Shark Tank, and Author of Mentor to Millions. He has launched over 20 businesses that have grown to over $100 million in sales each. Kevin has been involved in more than a dozen public companies and has launched over 500 products generating more than $5 billion in sales worldwide with iconic brands and celebrities such as Jack Lalanne, Tony Little, George Foreman, and the new I-Grow hair restoration product on QVC. He is the co-author of Mentor to Millions.

Introduction

> *There are those who look at things the way they are, and ask why?*
>
> *I dream of things that never were, and ask why not?*
>
> *George Bernard Shaw*

Perception! It goes beyond what we see hear, taste, and ultimately believe. It transcends our senses and ultimately determines our how and why.

Our perceptions shape how we process information ... how we reach conclusions ... how we form opinions ... our version of truth, our biases, our likes, our dislikes. Perception is our guide for how we make decisions and how we live our lives. It shapes who we hang out with and who we avoid. It guides us in what careers to seek, what jobs we take, and the type and location of the education we pursue.

Leaders and employers around the world grapple with the same issue Shakespeare's Juliet posed in the classic tale, "What's in a name? That which we call a rose, by any other name would smell as sweet." What is it in what we see, hear or experience that causes each of us to smile or react differently to the exact same experience? What's in a rose? Well, it depends!

Our brains never cease to amaze us. Through our eyes, ears, and nose, combined with our sense of touch and taste, scientists estimate that we absorb more than a thousand impressions per minute, which collectively tell us what is good, what is bad, what is dangerous and what is desirable.

We developed our sensory abilities as infants–our ability to see, hear, smell, taste, and touch. From those senses, we immediately began to formulate impressions of the world around us. As our abilities and our world expanded, our impressions either changed as we gathered new information, or they became embedded as "truths." And the longer those stereotypes and biases continued to be reinforced, we are told, they become absolutes. It is those truths that guide our thoughts, our conclusions, and our actions on a daily basis. What shoes to buy. Who to marry. Where to live. Which job to take.

"That looks like a good place to eat." "He seemed to be all right." "I believed it would help my career." According to an article in Psychology Today, we make about 35,000 decisions a day (Krochow, 2018). Many are small and insignificant, while some have a major impact on our lives. And all are guided by our perceptions.

Our perceptions are both a conscious and sub-conscious phenomenon. In some situations, we can trace why we do the things we do or make the choices we make. "I always knew I wanted to be a doctor because my father was a doctor." "I'm a Hindu because that's the way I was brought up."

Yet, in other situations, we are hard-pressed to explain why we shudder at the sight of lima beans or liver, or a colleague we are forced to work with. Many times, we simply can't explain why we feel the way we do or why we believe what we do. We know people who influenced our lives, but we don't always know why we like liberals versus conservatives, or why we're a cat person and not a dog person.

Our perceptions are our compass. They become embedded into our "instincts." They tell us where to go, where not to go, when to go, and if to go at all. "I could smell something fishy about him." "Something just didn't seem right." Perceptions also change. The more we know, the better we see things. Perhaps. Sometimes, those initial perceptions are "spot on" in our minds. "I knew from the first moment I saw him that he would be the one."

Sometimes, we alter our perceptions with new information. "I thought she would be a good fit until I watched her interact with her team." And sometimes, we hold doggedly to those initial perceptions despite new information. We can be blinded by our perceptions when the truth is in plain sight. "Despite the bad references, I'm going to go with him. I just feel like he is the best man for the job."

Our perceptions are heavily influenced by past experiences or our cultural upbringing, but sometimes by nothing more than a snap judgment or visceral reaction. "Why did I immediately dismiss her idea, even though it had merit?" And sometimes, those reactions are governed by our mood at the moment or our general disposition.

To what extent are our perceptions true, and when are they simply, well ... just our perceptions? We are told that perception is reality. Is it? It may be our reality, while it may not be others'. Where is that gap between perception and reality? At what point do we reach "truth?" While some people trust their gut based on first impressions, others are accused of "analysis/paralysis." Which approach gets us closer to what is "real?"

So, just what are those factors that shape our perceptions? And just how do they impact our lives? And, what is it that tells us when our perceptions are taking us down the wrong path? How do we differentiate what are our perceptions and what are the perceptions of others?

How do our truths shape and influence our ability to interact with others? Especially in a world that continues to shrink and become more diverse ... across cultures, across countries and across languages?

In his classic 2005 book, The World Is Flat, Thomas Friedman showcased the massive implications of the emerging age of globalism, fueled by technology and international trade. Our commerce is no longer only within our own community, or within our own country. Our interactions are no longer only with our neighbors or even our countrymen. Our languages, our customs, our currencies, and even our spiritual beliefs, are no longer the exclusive domain of our interactions. Ours is a global experience. At the time of this writing, the world is facing a global pandemic which showcases how our perception of this world being vast might have been off. Within months, what started in Wuhan, China became a global phenomenon and a global tragedy.

And therein lies a tale of technology and geo-economics that is fundamentally reshaping our lives–much, much more quickly than many people realize. It all happened while we were sleeping, or rather while we were focused on 9/11, the dot-com bust, and Enron–which even prompted some to wonder whether globalization was over. Actually, just the opposite was true, which is why it's time to wake up and prepare ourselves for this flat world, because others already are, and there is no time to waste.

The lackadaisical response to the coronavirus again teaches us that our perceptions affect our very being. The same technology that empowers our ability to connect can also be our biggest vulnerability.

So, how do we adapt to these new norms if we are to be a part of this new world order? The price of admission for today's workforce, and more importantly, today's leaders, requires a new and deeper sense of empathy, a new kind of understanding, in order to participate. And, it is our perceptions that are the vanguard of that adjustment. Reframing how we view others, and how others view us, must be the starting point. And it goes deeper than we may think.

Anil K. Seth, professor of Cognitive and Computational

Neuroscience at the University of Sussex in England, reminds us in his TED Talk (2017) and in other presentations that our perceptions go much deeper than those we garner at a conscious level. The manifestations of our perceptions may reside on the tips of our tongues, but their roots are deeply embedded in our subconscious. It is not sufficient that we merely mouth those perceptual adjustments that are "politically correct." If we are to truly adapt, we must examine what we believe, and why.

Which brings us to the fundamental purpose of this book, and its ancillary products. We share Professor Seth's perspective. It is our belief that we must reshape our perceptions, both consciously and unconsciously, to become more responsive to this emerging multi-cultural, multi-language world in which we are now living.

As a contributor, as a leader, and as a fellow human being in this global information economy, we must know when our perceptions are working for us, and when they're working against us. We must allow our perceptive abilities to grow and keep up with these changes that are occurring at a dizzying pace.

So, can we "monitor" our perceptions, and perhaps guide them towards where we want to go, and away from where we don't want to go? Absolutely. We can choose what to watch on television, who and who not to associate with. We can gravitate toward those who share our beliefs, and we can explore and learn from those who think differently. That is the foundation of our growth.

Can we "change" or "alter" our perceptions? Again, the answer is yes. We can cultivate our taste for scotch or red wine. We can learn that accents are no indication of intelligence, or that Northerners do not have personas that are cold and impersonal.

We can even rethink and reshape our beliefs about capitalism, socialism, or our own political or spiritual beliefs. The more we learn, the more we examine, the more our perceptions change.

So, does this mean we can "manage" our perceptions? We're three for three here. Once again, the answer is yes. We see what we see. We hear what we hear. We feel what we feel. That is just life coming at us with us having some, but little, control over all that we encounter. And again, some are happening at a conscious level, while others happen unconsciously. But we can control how we think about those things.

How we perceive, not what we perceive, is what influences how and what we think and believe, which, in turn, influences our behaviors. If we are to engage others both of our own and other cultures, it is essential that we become more cognizant, more self-aware of our own perceptions and those of others. It is the archetypical "walk a mile in my shoes." It is the knowledge that before we can meaningfully engage, I must know where you are coming from; and you must know where I'm coming from.

Our objective is to introduce you to a new and practical approach in which to be more aware of how you perceive; how your perceptions impact your behaviors; how they impact the behaviors of those around you; and, provide you a foundation from which to manage that process. Ours is a simple premise:

Our perceptions are a powerful and, in many cases, subliminal force that play a major role in shaping our attitudes, our behaviors and our interactions with others. Therefore, to work more effectively in a global, multi-cultural environment, a more conscious approach to being aware of, and better managing our perceptions is essential.

Our journey to test and validate that premise is reflected in this book, and a set of companion tools. To outline our findings, we have organized the book into those three basic components:

Part I is to examine the major factors that shape our perceptions ... that influence what we believe and why we believe.

Part II is to examine the impact those factors have in shaping our behaviors ... how we interact with others, and the implications of those interactions.

and,

Part III is to examine a new practical approach to how you govern your perceptions, and introduce you to some tools to help you do just that.

Can we shape and alter our thinking to allow our perceptions to help us to become more effective as decision makers, as judges of character, as leaders in this new world order? Can that which is such a uniquely individualized and deeply embedded trait of our human condition be shaped? The answer is yes! And it is our intent to demonstrate just that.

Welcome to our journey!

Part I:

How Our Perceptions
Are Formed

Chapter One:
Perception and Culture

> *One must respect traditions and culture, but it must not determine how we interact with others.*
>
> *Nelson Mandela*

Introduction

We do not come out of the womb with a predisposition toward how to view and interpret our surroundings. We begin with a blank slate. We are then imprinted ... by our parents, our relatives, our neighborhood, our church, our community, and the region where we live–in essence, our culture–with impressions of how we are supposed to behave.

Our culture is the first dynamic that begins to shape what is good and what is bad. It is the most pervasive influence in shaping the way we view the world, especially in the early stages of our life. The behavioral patterns we learn as infants follow us into our childhoods and, in many instances, into our adult lives to shape our thoughts, our beliefs and our behaviors. Even those times when we were rebellious adolescents, questioning everything, we did so within a certain, culturally acceptable set of parameters.

Culture is defined as "the behaviors, beliefs and characteristics of a particular social, ethnic or age group." That is the original imprint that shapes every facet of our lives. Even our innermost private thoughts are influenced by what we are supposed to think.

Think about when you greet a stranger. Do you shake hands

and, in your native language, say, "How do you do?" Or do you bow? Or do you greet them with a different ritualistic custom of your native land or region? When someone behaves or even dresses in a certain manner, is the behavior questionable or acceptable? A woman wearing a miniskirt in Brazil would be viewed very differently if she were in Saudi Arabia.

Our culture shapes what we think and how we think. Sometimes, it becomes difficult to separate what we think from what we are supposed to think. It also shapes what we value. Some cultures place a high value on teachers, healers, and the lessons of the elderly, while others place a much higher value on individualism, consumerism or "finding your own way."

Culture serves a valuable purpose. It is a pillar of human society. As such, it creates a framework within which human beings exist and interact. It establishes the guidelines and parameters that allow us to survive and succeed. But, where is the line? At what point do we allow our culture or society to dictate what we think and how we perceive? And, at what point do we factor our individual thoughts or beliefs into that equation?

Those are our questions.

Author and Executive Director Emeritus at University of California Berkeley's International House, Joe Lurie, in his book, A Mind-Opening Journey Across Culture, cites numerous behaviors that are acceptable in some cultures, while considered strange or even offensive in others.

For example, while eye contact in Western cultures is considered to be a sign of candor and confidence, in other cultures, in Africa for example, students avoid making eye contact with a person of authority or an elder, to show respect.

Or how, in some cultures, it's considered perfectly normal to see men casually holding hands, while in many Western cultures, that type of behavior would provoke immediate implications of homosexuality.

Our perceptions are grounded in our cultural origins. In many Asian cultures, street vendors or other merchants use calculators to negotiate the price of their offerings. "The calculator," cites retired international business executive G. Ross Kelly, "is their way of challenging the price of an item without offending the individual. Focusing on the calculator and not the individual allows you to negotiate aggressively without being disrespectful."

> *We do not see things as they are; we see things as we are.*
>
> **Anais Nin**

The Center of Intercultural Competence, an international agency that provides training and assessment services to foster intercultural competence, cites a variety of examples of how everyday gestures viewed very positively in one culture can do just the opposite in another. For example, in Africa, saying to a female friend she has put on weight can be a compliment, whereas in Europe, North America and Australia, this would be considered insulting.

They further remind us that the physical gestures such as a thumbs up, or the thumb and forefinger used to form the letter O in some cultures means "everything is A-OK," and in others it means something sexual.

Or did you ever have a conversation with someone from India who shook their head to say "yes," but in your language, the shake meant "no"?

In their training and assessment programs, The Center for Intercultural Competence describes hundreds of verbal and non-verbal gestures that differ from country to country and culture to culture, and how each can either foster credibility and respect, or ridicule and insult.

In a number of their studies, the Center concludes that Americans and people from Western cultures tend to have the biggest difficulties in working across cultures. Any culture that places a high premium on individualism, such as those countries, they say, is particularly challenged in their ability to understand someone else's point of view.

Perhaps the biggest challenge when it comes to perceptions across cultures is avoiding cultural stereotypes. Typically fostered by media and entertainment sources, stereotypes can simplify our thinking and marginalize the individuals that fall prey to them.

There are cultures in which black males can be associated with criminal activities, or Muslims can be linked to terrorism, or blonde females can be portrayed as ditzy or even dumb. Unless we look beyond these stereotypes, they can be the first perception we have upon meeting anyone who falls into one of the subjected categories. Stereotypes have the ability to hinder our perception and block our view of others. Stereotypes are used as mental shortcuts and defensive mechanisms, typically without us being aware of our own inclination towards stereotyping certain groups of people.

As entrepreneur and billionaire Naveen Jain commented in a podcast interview, "I think it's time we put the stereotypes aside, and get to know the real person" (Hamilton, n.d.).

> *Your assumptions are your windows on the world. Scrub them off every once in a while, or the light won't come in.*
>
> **Alan Alda**

One additional thought on the topic of biases, stereotypes and cultural differences ... while the cultural differences of others can be glaringly obvious to us, we can be blind to our own cultural idiosyncrasies.

At an international training and team building conference, participants were organized into teams and, as group exercises, were given various challenges or problems to solve. Each team consisted of corporate professionals from the U.S., Japan, Brazil, India, Africa and Europe. In one of these exercises, the team leader, who was from the U.S., said to his team members while looking at his Japanese counterpart, "Remember the K.I.S.S. principle: Keep it simple stupid!"

The phrase, commonly known in U.S. business circles, was taken quite literally by the Japanese team member. Believing his American counterpart had called him stupid, the Japanese team member was highly offended and requested to be reassigned to another team. He told the conference coordinator the American was "arrogant and condescending, and called him stupid!"

What is said, and how it's said, in one culture can be perceived very differently in another. "Cultural awareness" means not only being aware of other cultures, but your own as well. Being aware of others' culture and customs is critical. But, an equally important question to ask yourself is, "How are my customs and practices different from those I'm engaging with?"

There is a Zen parable of two tadpoles swimming in a pond. Suddenly, one turns into a frog and leaves the pond. When the frog returns to the water, the second tadpole asks, "Where did you go?"

"I went to a dry place," answers the frog.

"What is dry?" asks the second tadpole.

"Dry is where there is no water," says the frog.

The second tadpole then asks, "And what is 'water?'"

"You don't know what 'water' is?!" the frog replies in disbelief. "It's all around you! Can't you see it?"

Self-examination of your own traditions, values and behaviors is key to understanding how they differ from those of other countries and cultures.

> **All colors look the same in the dark.**
>
> **Francis Bacon**

The earliest beginnings of the need for a more culturally sensitive workforce began to emerge in the early 21st century. With the rise of the Internet as a business transaction tool, combined with the increase of global business practices, cultural sensitivity gained focus. Both business leaders and academicians began chronicling how cultural differences were beginning to impact international trade and commerce.

Thus began the rising need for a means of measuring one's cultural intelligence or CQ.

The first publication of cultural intelligence was written by Christopher Earley, Soon Ang and Joo-Seng Tan, entitled CQ:

Developing Cultural Intelligence. Their work, among other research, led The Harvard Gazette to cite cultural intelligence as a core capability essential for success in twenty-first century business (Mitchell, 2014).

David Livermore is president and partner at the Cultural Intelligence Center and author of numerous books on the subject, among them being Leading with Cultural Intelligence.

In it, Livermore says the number one predictor of success is not your IQ, but your CQ. He defines cultural intelligence as the capability to function effectively in a variety of cultural contexts, including national, ethnic, organization, and generational. He describes the dramatic shift towards a more multi-cultural existence, saying, "Fifty years ago, we all were surrounded by people who looked, believed and saw the world like we do. Now one billion tourist visas are issued annually, with the number rising."

Livermore defines four capabilities that constitute your cultural intelligence, or CQ:

CQ Drive (motivation), which he describes as one's interest and confidence in functioning effectively in culturally diverse settings.

CQ Knowledge (cognition), which he says is your knowledge about how cultures are similar and different.

CQ Strategy (meta-cognition), defined as how one can comprehend culturally diverse experiences. Can you plan effectively in light of those cultural differences?

and,

CQ Action (behavior), one's capability to appropriately adjust their behavior to different cultures, i.e., having a flexible repertoire of responses to suit various situations while still remaining true to yourself.

How would you rate yourself in those four categories? Adapt, Change or Respect?

OK, so what do we do with this raised awareness of how we view our own culture versus the differences of others? The questions that invariably arise in the examination of cultures include, "Should I adapt to those customs of others? Or, should I insist they change their customs to mine? Or, should I merely tolerate the differences?"

The answer is none of the above. Rather than require anyone to change or adjust their cultural behaviors, the cultural scientists tell us simply to respect and celebrate the differences. Tolerating different cultural backgrounds is a step in the right direction. However, tolerance is not always optimal. In fact, tolerance usually means that you are simply putting up with something that is undesirable. Cultural competence goes beyond "putting up with" differences and instead involves being appreciative, affirming, and inclusive of all cultural backgrounds.

As Dan Gainor, Executive Director of the Culture and Media Institute says, acknowledge them, honor them, learn from them. "The more I sense that you are aware of our differences, he says, the more I embrace you."

The great American author and philosopher, Mark Twain said, "Travel is hazardous to prejudice, bigotry and narrow-mindedness . . . ."

Whether your education of different cultures is via travel or via the Internet, it is crucial to collaborating or leading others who may see things through a different cultural lens than yours.

Conclusion

Our culture is at the heart of what we learn from the very beginnings of our lives. From what we think, to how we feel and what we value, the culture in which we are born and raised serves as our foundation.

We are taught, even as adults, to seek out the "ingroupers," those who think and believe as we do; and to avoid the "outgroupers," those who don't. We develop what behavioral scientists refer to as ethnocentrism, the belief that ours is the superior culture; our way is the right way. And we make value judgments accordingly.

But what happens as our world gets smaller and our cultures begin to intermingle with one another? As technology and globalism bring our cultures closer together, we are taught not to judge other cultures that have different customs and traditions than our own, but to study them, to learn from them.

We learned that the foundation of virtually every culture that is different and has different beliefs or values from ours is rooted in pragmatism. We learned that different people and regions around the world find different ways to solve the same problems. Our culture at the time and place of our birth is most likely very different than the culture that shapes the way we live and work today. Our world is smaller and more heterogeneous.

Consider the analogy of a bi-racial child who inherits the blood and genetic makeup of two separate races. That child does not have the frame of reference to view the world exclusively through one racial or cultural lens, or the other. Theirs is a view that is uniquely different from either of their parents and others within their social circle, since they may be perceived as "different" due to the way they look.

The cultures of the world are on a similar path.

Given the wonders of technology, American culture is being influenced by Japanese culture, and vice versa. African culture is being influenced by European culture and vice versa. And while many customs in various cultures hold steadfastly to their roots, others are being reshaped and influenced by the media, by travel and by technology.

What you believed to be true when you were a child may no longer be the case. What you believed before you traveled to Africa or the United States for the first time may no longer exist. Our cultures and our perceptions that were shaped by those earlier beliefs are fluid and continue to evolve.

As a result, our challenges are: One, to stay abreast of what is culturally chic and what has become passé; two, to know where our cultures end and others begin; and three, to honor the difference.

Chapter Two:
Perception and Spirituality

Make your own Bible. Select and collect all the words and sentences that in all your readings have been to you like the blast of a trumpet.

Ralph Waldo Emerson

Introduction

Welcome to the topic that dares to venture deeper into the realm of our personal beings than any other we explore ... our spiritualism. But before we dive off the deep end into this topic, we should probably establish a common definition of just what we mean when we say "spiritualism."

To fully explore this delicate and highly personal topic, we consulted with a wide array of experts, ranging from social scientists to philosophers, clergymen (and women), and, dare we say, "spiritualists." And, as you probably would have predicted, we received a variety of views and beliefs. The spectrum ranges from those who regard themselves to be "highly religious," to those who are "turned off" by religion and pursue a more "spiritual" path, to those who discard the religious or spiritual element altogether, thus relying on that which can be seen or touched in the natural world for their guidance. Whichever spiritual or religious avenue you choose to embrace or not embrace, the evidence is clear that the phenomenon plays a role in shaping our views and beliefs.

When we asked ten people, we received ten different answers, which immediately told us we needed to refine the scope of our exploration of the linkage between our perceptions and our spirituality. So, for the purposes of this discussion, we're going to once again reduce the many facets of this word into an admittedly overly simplistic definition:

> **Spiritualism: *That inner voice that guides us in our beliefs, our attitudes and our actions.***

With that working definition stated, this is not about religion. Religion is indeed one of the various vehicles from which to exercise your spirituality, but the two should not be confused. Whether it be your beliefs in an organized religion, from Christianity, to Islam, to Buddhism, to Hinduism, or be it meditation, astrology, or anything else in between, we're talking about that inner compass that guides you and your attitudes and behaviors toward others.

With that distinction established, there is a second element that must be factored into the equation of how perception shapes your spirituality, which is the strength of that conviction. How strongly do you embrace your spirituality? For example, if I'm a Christian, but a lukewarm Christian with questions or doubts about my religious faith, that can affect my thinking, and therefore, my perceptions. But the strength of our spirituality tends to shift over time.

Our spirituality is perhaps the most deeply felt phenomenon of our being, heavily influenced by our perceptions, and goes through an evolution of sorts. That evolution typically occurs in four major phases. They are:

Phase I – Inheriting the Beliefs of Our Family
Phase II – Examination of those Beliefs
Phase III – Resolving Your Beliefs and finally,
Phase IV – Personalizing Your Beliefs

How we go through these phases in our spiritual growth, and the role our perceptions play in the process, is the subject of this chapter. Ready to explore?

Phase I – Inheriting Our Spirituality

When we are born into the environment of our families and community, we typically "inherit" and adapt the spiritual beliefs of those around us. Those who grow up in a Jewish household are taught to assume the Jewish faith ... as do Christians, Muslims, Buddhists or even non-believers. We inherit the faith, as well as the strength of the convictions of that faith, and the behaviors. If my family is of the Muslim faith and attends the mosque regularly, I inherit those same attitudes and behaviors. If my family is Catholic and goes to Mass every morning, that becomes my norm. If, by contrast, they show little or no interest in their own spirituality, I am inclined to mimic those same behaviors.

Roger Paul Neyman is on the faculty at Wilmette Institute where he teaches a course called "Science, Religion and the Baha'i Faith," and is also the author of the book, *Fostering Hope: Harmonizing Science, Religion and the Arts*. He describes how, at this stage, it is your eyes and ears that are guiding your spirituality, not your heart or some innate inner faith.

In the initial stages of our spiritual development, it is our attitudes and the behaviors of others that are guiding our spirituality. When we have yet to internalize our beliefs, we tend to look to others. Our perceptions are externally focused.

Phase II – Examination of Our Beliefs

As we age, at some point in our spiritual evolution, be that at age fourteen or forty, we begin to become curious about those spiritual beliefs we inherited. We observe other forms of spirituality and begin to compare. We delve deeper into the core of those beliefs. We ask questions. And at some point, the response, "Because" is no longer sufficient as the answer. We undertake a more thorough analysis of the various aspects of the spiritual teachings we inherited; hence, we go through a phase of "examination."

Richard J. Foster's *Celebration of Discipline: The Path to Spiritual Growth* is hailed by many as the best modern book on Christian spirituality with millions of copies sold since its original publication in 1978. In *Celebration of Discipline*, Foster explores how he reached a point of spiritual bankruptcy in his own life, and how the perception of his spirituality began to change during that time.

He was well versed in the spiritual teachings of his childhood, so much that he became a minister. But in his early ministry, he found himself, as he described it, doing little more than mouthing the words of those early teachings. Not knowing if he was having second thoughts about his faith or if he was simply missing something, he began to seek guidance. He consulted with other ministers and lay people. He also attended the services of many of those other ministers to critically examine their message and their methods.

After months of examination, Foster's faith was renewed. He rediscovered his passion for his beliefs and began to inject that sense of passion into his message. His period of examination brought him back to his earlier teachings, only this time, it was not the spirituality he had inherited. It was his own.

His intense examination was guided by his perceptions of others, but his resolution was a result of his own perceptions.

Those examinations invariably take us in one of two directions; we may reaffirm or solidify those beliefs we were taught, like Richard Foster. In the Christian faith, that is when you hear phrases like being "born again." Or, conversely, we can have a change of heart and take our spiritual beliefs in a different direction. This is typically what's happened when you hear of Catholics converting to Judaism. Or Christians converting to Islam, or even individuals leaving organized religion altogether, to become atheist or agnostic.

This is a phase in our spiritual evolution in which we also begin to more clearly understand that spirituality and religion are two different things, with spirituality being understood as that sense of inner peace and guidance that we all seek, and religion being one of the sources that provides us that inner peace and guidance.

Further, it is a phase that can last for years and even decades.

Phase III – Resolving Your Spirituality

The third phase toward embracing our spirituality is when we begin to reconcile any differences or conflicts, if any. Whether it is a reaffirmation of the spiritual beliefs we inherited from our family, or whether it moves in a completely different direction, this third phase is where our spiritual beliefs truly become our own, as opposed to those which were given to us.

Steven Simpson, a technology executive for an American firm, spent much of his time in Europe and Africa opening new subsidiaries for his company. Originally from the Midwest and born into a Catholic family, Steven described himself a "moderate" Catholic, still in the habit of going to Mass every Sunday when his job would allow.

During one of his visits to Nigeria, Steven was exposed to the Yoruba religion and found himself comparing the indigenous beliefs to the Catholic beliefs he had practiced since childhood. Though born and raised Catholic, the executive acknowledged he had just enough questions about his faith to allow himself the freedom to explore other alternatives.

He described his experience from his study of the Yoruba beliefs as being less "religious" and more grounded in universal principles of doing good. He expressed no desires to convert to another religion, but found himself enthralled by how the Yoruba beliefs transcended the religious dogma he had been accustomed to.

For the first time, at the age of fifty-eight, he said, he discovered the true meaning of what he had failed to grasp through the teachings of the Catholic church. He maintains his relationship with the Catholic church and its teachings, but now with a renewed understanding of what he had been missing.

Whether we describe ourselves as religious or spiritual, or neither, that ultimate resolution of our spirituality tends to bring us an inner peace we had not previously experienced. Our perceptions become even more internalized.

Phase IV – Personalization of Your Beliefs

So, what is the difference between Phase III and Phase IV? The short answer is the difference between finding your spirituality, and *living* that spirituality in the way you think, behave and act toward others. Phase III is about what you believe. Phase IV is about how you live. The journey of finding your true beliefs about your spirituality can be a long and arduous one. The journey of modifying your attitudes and behaviors to reflect those beliefs can be equally so.

We all know of individuals who describe themselves as virtuous and spiritual, or religious, yet their actions don't seem to reflect their expressed values or beliefs. Whether they resolve themselves to the religious or spiritual beliefs of their childhood, or embrace a new set of spiritual beliefs later in life, or choose another path, exhibiting those beliefs can be a challenge.

So, what may be the relevance of this when it comes to perception, and more importantly, the issues of leadership or success in the workplace? So glad you asked.

In his best-seller, *The 7 Habits of Highly Effective People*, author Stephen R. Covey cites spiritual renewal as one of those habits that are essential to effective leadership. He says, whatever your spiritual beliefs, and whatever combinations of perception guided you to those beliefs, one's spiritual beliefs or non-beliefs, and the degree to their behavior is congruent with those beliefs, is regarded as one of the highest forms of leadership.

A principle-centered leader, Covey says, finds and instills in its employees a sense of meaning, asking questions, such as,

❑ *What is our greater purpose?*

❑ *What are our values and ethical principles?*

❑ *What will be our legacy?*

The principle-centered leader strives for a workplace that is truly a community, consisting of people with shared traditions, values, and beliefs.

Each of the four phases we go through in defining and living our spirituality are guided by perhaps the widest array of perceptions. From observing our family, our friends and our community, to examining our own inner-most thoughts, to searching the heavens, it is what we see, hear and feel, that ultimately takes us there.

> *Your physical eyes can see one thing, but it's how your heart understands that allows you to perceive the world around you.*
>
> **Author Unknown**

How Our Spirituality Influences Our Behaviors

Our spiritual beliefs vary in dramatically divergent ways. There are those who adhere to organized religions, be they Muslims, Buddhists, Christians or Hindu. There are others who disdain organized religions of any sort, and adhere to a broader spiritual belief. Then there are those who discount the very existence of a higher power and look to the powers of the human spirit. The labels abound, from religious to atheist, to agnostic, to spiritual, to none of the above. This thesis is not to advocate or even acknowledge any particular spiritual belief. It is to merely acknowledge that those beliefs, whatever they may be, have a significant influence on how and what we perceive.

There are studies, for example, of how one's spirituality comes to the forefront when confronted with peril, while there are other studies that conclude the exact opposite.

It appears the most striking commonality in those studies is not the nature of one's belief, but the strength of their conviction in what they believe. Be they strongly religious, agnostic, atheist, or any of the other labels that are used, how strongly we believe tends to impact our perceptions more than what we believe.

While our spiritual or religious beliefs can enable us to resolve the uncertainties or ambiguities in our lives, they can also hamper our abilities to engage others if we are unable to accept others who have different beliefs. Knowing the impact our spiritual beliefs have on our perceptions and our behaviors, our challenge is to (a) find and embrace those beliefs that serve as our own well-being, and (b) be tolerant and accepting of those whose beliefs differ from our own.

In the words of Swami Krishnananda, in his book, *The Path to Freedom: Mastering The Art of Total Perception*, "When freedom is given to a person who does not know how to exercise freedom properly, it becomes a cause of bondage."

Spirituality – The Sixth Sense

When you join your friends for dinner at a nice restaurant, you experience the sights, the sounds, the smells, the tastes, all of the senses of the evening. But, none of those by themselves interpret the experience as "a great evening." It is the overlay of spirituality, scientists tell us, that wraps the sum of those individual parts into the total experience. We connect different elements at that dinner table and interpret them based on our individual mood, thoughts, feelings and interpretations. That is why the very same dinner can be interpreted as wonderful, mediocre or downright awful by different individuals.

In his book, *Science and Spirituality*, author Pilani V. Krishnamurthy debunks the long-held myth that science and spirituality are incompatible with one another. He further describes how it is our spirituality that converts raw perceptions into a more holistic experience.

When the astronauts of Apollo 11 went to the moon, Neil Armstrong and Buzz Aldrin, scientifically and without emotion, described the moon's motionless atmosphere, the powdery nature of its soil, the structure of its craters and moon rocks and its barren horizons. But it was their spirituality that described their collective perceptions as 'a heavenly, majestic setting.'

It is our spiritualism that goes beyond the physical elements of our perceptions, to give them meaning and context.

Krishnamurthy describes perception and spirituality as two complementary facets of our intellectual aspirations, neither of which can be ignored. While science is universally accepted as the arbiter of truth, spirituality is not, and is therefore often overlooked. For many, it is their spirituality that gives scientific findings their true meaning and purpose, whereas others work diligently to prevent their beliefs about spirituality influence or contaminate their scientific findings.

Perceptual Filter

In Encyclopedia of Identity, perceptual filtering is described as the process of taking in new information and interpreting it according to prior experiences and cultural norms. People use these perceptual filters to help reduce uncertainty about new experiences. As the term suggests, perceptual filtering regards people's perceptions, the way people take in and make sense of information, about the social world. Our spirituality is one of those perceptual filters, which gives meaning to what we are perceiving and that which ties the mosaic together.

Conclusion

Wherever you may be on your road to developing and ultimately personalizing your beliefs about your spirituality, your perceptions have been traveling that road with you. The path we travel to define our spirituality creates our most deeply held beliefs and therefore should be a personal one.

It is also one of the most influential. Our beliefs about our faith or spirituality influence what we believe and how we interact with others. Wherever you reside on the spectrum, from highly religious to non-believer, get to know your spiritual beliefs. Know how they influence your actions toward others. Our perceptions shape our actions; and our beliefs about our spirituality, for some, are perhaps our most sacred and deeply felt of those perceptions. Hence, our beliefs about our spirituality can deeply influence our performance and success in the workplace.

Chapter Three
Perception and Gender

I frequently consult my wife on many issues.
She sees the world through a lens I do not possess.

Mahatma Gandhi

Introduction

*T*wo strangers, a man and woman, were visiting an art gallery and found themselves standing next one another studying a painting of an old country estate, replete with an elderly man sitting in a rocking chair on the front porch of a mansion, with various barns and outbuildings serving as its background.

The woman, without prompting, commented, "What a beautiful painting. So serene and peaceful. A beautiful blend of man and nature."

The man commented in response, "That barn looks like it is in dire need of a paint job."

These two individuals, one a man and one a woman, see two completely different things in the same painting. They see the same things in the painting, but they're drawn to different aspects, summarizing the artwork in two completely different ways.

Is it that one is an art aficionado and one is not? Is it that one is a fan of nature and one is not? Is it that the man has an affinity for the integrity of structures?

Or, is it that one is a man and one is a woman?

What role does our gender play in what we see or don't see? Do women innately see things differently than men? Or are they trained or conditioned by society to do so? Whichever it may be, the differences are evident … in the way we react to different stimuli, the way we speak and the way we behave. And how do those differences play out in the workplace? Or, across cultures.

The physiological differences between males and females are well documented, including differences in their brains. But do those known differences translate into men and women viewing the world differently? Or, is that a societal phenomenon?

The answers to those questions are the subject of this chapter.

We often hear of "gender bias." We know of studies that show women are viewed differently, treated differently and paid differently than men. We know of the predominance of the number of men compared to women in executive positions in businesses. The numbers may vary slightly from region to region, from country to country, but the trends are the same.

Our objective here is not to make the case for gender equality in the workplace, but to understand how those biases and differences originate. How does our gender affect what we see, how we see it, and what we do about it? And, how do those perceptions affect our performance in the workplace?

That is our quest.

Caveat

This chapter does not address, nor should it be confused with, the issue of gender perception. That is a topic, for example, that has become somewhat trendy lately, given the emergence of the LGBTQ movement. The subject of gender perception is about how we define and classify genders, which, before the aforementioned trends, used to be a simple task. For example, some individuals now use different pronouns on their social media profiles (they/them/theirs rather than she/her/hers or he/him/his). This opens up a whole new set of challenges for employers and human resource professionals. But this is a topic we will leave to the behavioral scientists who appear to be in dogged pursuit of those answers.

Our focus will be limited to the how and why of the different male and female views of the world and the workplace.

Its Origins

We know that women see the world through a different lens than their male counterparts, and we know that the reasons why are a function of both nature and nurture. Physiologically, the male brain is structurally different than the female brain which is a significant factor. But what about the nurture component … that which we learn from our parents, our communities and our cultures? With nature serving as the catalyst that gets things started, nurture, our culture, tends to take those distinctions to another level, dating back to the Stone Age.

So, the root causes of why the two genders see the world differently are not your boss, your spouse or your co-workers. Those root causes begin with your parents, who form the basic genetic makeup that determines your gender, and therefore, the genetic foundation of your brain.

There have been endless studies and books written about how the male and female brains are genetically different.

Dr. Louanne Brinzendine is an American scientist, a neuropsychiatrist, a researcher and professor at the University of California, San Francisco. Brinzendine wrote two separate publications that illustrate those differences. Her first, a *New York Times* best-seller, was called *The Female Brain;* and then her follow-up published in 2010 was called, appropriately enough, *The Male Brain.* In each, she guides us through how the brains of each gender differ, and how those differences shape our behaviors … from the time we're infants, as children, as adolescents and into our adulthoods.

Brizendine concludes that women's perceptions and behaviors are different from those of men due, in large measure, to hormones. In her publications, she cites the hormones that govern the female brain, including estrogen, progesterone, and testosterone, and then traces those hormones back to the elements of the brain that transmit those hormones, including the prefrontal cortex, the hypothalamus, and the amygdala.

Given the structural differences between the male and female brains, which are well-documented, she cites these hormonal flows as being the foundation of the different perceptions and behaviors between the two genders.

Dr. Diane Hamilton conducted an interview with Tom Peters, the iconic co-author of the 1980s business classic, *In Search of Excellence.* As it turns out, Peters is an avid student and advocate of the differences between male and female brains. Citing Brizendine's book, *The Female Brain,* he recalled an article he had read on the subject regarding Duke University basketball coach Mike Krzyzewski. Referencing an article from the *Sunday*

Times magazine section, he described how the legendary coach, often referred to as Coach K, would bring his wife to all the team meetings. The reason, he said, was because his wife could see things about what's going on in players' lives that he would never see. "She can smell a girlfriend problem from 100 yards away or she can smell a level of distraction," Peters said. "Men don't physiologically see those things. I thought it was a fascinating observation," he concluded.

Simon Baron-Cohen, a professor of psychology and psychiatry at Cambridge University, authored *The Essential Difference: Men, Women and the Extreme Male Brain*. Baron-Cohen's work, which examines the genetic wiring of the brain, cites many of the same findings. Throughout the publication, the author provides ample scientific evidence behind the innate gender differences in the make-up of the brain.

In yet another ample body of work, the University of Pennsylvania conducted a series of studies that looked at specific behavioral differences between the male and female brain, and how that shaped their differences in perception. The results of the study were published in 2013 and were conducted by Dr. Ragini Verma, Professor in Biomedical Image Analysis and others at the university. Titled "Sex differences in the structural connectome of the human brain," the study showed that, for example, while men tend to be better at focusing on a single task at hand, like cycling or navigating directions, women tend to demonstrate superior memory and social cognition skills, making them more equipped for multitasking and creating solutions that work for a group (Grant, 2013).

University researchers found that in the cerebrum, the largest part of the brain, females displayed greater connectivity between their left and right brains, whereas males, on the other hand, displayed greater connectivity within each hemisphere of their brains. In contrast, the opposite was true in the cerebellum, the part of the brain that plays a major role in motor control. Males, they concluded, displayed greater connections between the hemispheres of their brains, and females displayed greater connections within each hemisphere of their brains (Grant). Got it? I know; it can be tough to follow.

The bottom line goes back to the title of the article written by Bob Grant about the study in *The Scientist,* "Male and Female Brains Wired Differently." Men and women's brains are wired differently, which accounts for the many different behavioral attributes of males and females, and how they perceive.

These findings were consistent with other studies the group performed in which females outperformed males on attention, word and face memory, and social cognition tests; and males performed better on spatial processing and sensorimotor speed.

From the womb to adulthood, these innate differences appear to remain consistent.

Another corollary study was led by Dr. Israel Abramov, a Rhodesian born professor of psychology, cognition and behavioral neuroscience at the City University of New York (CUNY) Graduate School. He and a group of researchers from CUNY's Brooklyn campus and Hunter College conducted a series of studies to determine if those innate differences at birth carry over into adulthood. Their focus was not on the differences in the physical attributes of the two genders, but the perceptual differences, such as sight, sound and smell.

In summary, the studies revealed that, as adults, the distinctions remain.

The findings showed a variety of behavioral differences, that the researchers said may appear seemingly obscure, but demonstrate the differences between the two. For example, men tend to focus on the mouth in conversing with another, and are more likely to be distracted by movement behind that person than their female counterparts. Women, in contrast, tend to shift their gaze between a speaker's eyes and body, and frequently shift their gaze to other objects while conversing.

In another study, the researchers found that females are much more perceptive of colors, and other subtleties in color changes. Their male counterparts tend to place less focus on color distinctions and when asked to describe color variations, they require much more time to differentiate between colors than their female counterparts.

Abramov explained how these distinctions are linked to specific sets of thalamic neurons in the brain's primary visual cortex, and controlled by male sex hormones called androgens when the embryo is developing into a fetus. This further suggests, the psychologist said, that testosterone plays a major role, somehow leading to different connectivity between males and females.

The researchers also found similar distinctions in other sensory areas. For example, women tend to have a better tuned sense of hearing and smell than their male counterparts. The studies concluded that, in most cases, females had better sensitivity, and were able to discriminate and categorize odors better than males.

These innate distinctions between the male and female brain set the stage for another element of the brain that serves as a critical linkage between nature and nurture, and how they combine to impact our perceptions.

The Reticular Activator

Marilee B. Sprenger is a professor at Aurora University in Aurora, Illinois. Her studies focus on brain-based teaching, learning and memory, and she is the author of *Learning and Memory: The Brain in Action*. Sprenger says the major linkage from our brains to our perceptions is called the reticular activating system (RAS).

The reticular activating system (RAS), is a set of connected nuclei that reside in the thalamus of the brain and is responsible for regulating wakefulness and sleep-wake transitions. It is the same device that "programs" what you see, what you hear, what you feel, etc.

Sprenger tells us the reticular activator is the portal through which nearly all information enters the brain. (Smells, she tells us, are the lone exception. She explains they go directly into your brain's emotional area.) The RAS is, in essence, the gatekeeper of the brain; determining what is or is not going to get access to the full calculating power of your brain. Depending on how it's programmed, it determines what you pay attention to and what you don't; what arouses you and what does not. etc.

As a survival mechanism, the RAS is what causes you to respond to your name or anything that threatens your survival. It is also the mechanism that highlights information that you may need immediately, for example, if you're scanning through files looking for a particular file. It is the reticular activator that highlights the name of that file.

Did you ever read about something, like the name of a remote island you had never heard of, and within the next week, you heard that island mentioned in the news or in conversation? That's the reticular activator at work.

That "programming" function, Sprenger says, occurs both consciously and sub-consciously. We inherit many of our messages from our parents and our communities subconsciously through teachings, messages or modeled behaviors. They are imprinted into our memories as facts or as universal truths.

If I observe my father wake up and go to work every morning, my reticular activator stores that memory as a universal truth. And if I see someone else's father do something that varies from that truth, it immediately triggers my memory.

Sprenger tells us you can also consciously program your thinking to believe specific things. Conscious efforts, labeled as anything from "mind control" to hypnosis, to motivational talks, are increasing ways to attempt to program the reticular activator to believe certain things.

These efforts are grounded in the belief that what your mind believes is a primary determinant in your behavior. Which brings us back to the differences in how the brains of males and females are wired differently, thus serving as the foundation for how they perceive differently.

So, Which is it … Nature or Nurture? Or Both?

By virtue of our differences in the make-up of our brains, we are pre-dispositioned to perceive the world in different ways. Then, employing that combination of nature and nurture, the reticular activator is the programming device in our brains that tells us what to pay attention to and what to ignore … essentially, how and what to perceive. That is where nurture takes over.

From their very birth, we begin to imprint our children with what it means to be a boy or a girl. We dress them in different colors. We decorate their rooms differently. We buy them different toys to play with. We even take them to different areas on the playground.

Whatever variances may exist across different cultures, one commonality tends to be common to them all. That is how we distinguish the two genders and begin the process of shaping their perceptions accordingly.

That view is further driven by the physical differences between the two genders. Boys, though slower to develop, grow to become physically larger in stature and stronger, with messages of being a protector, a provider, or in some respects, dominant. In some cultures, such as the U.S., girls play with dolls and play house in preparation for being acculturated to the eventuality of childbearing. Their messages are far different than boys.

With that societal introduction, our children's reticular activators immediately go to work. Females are programmed to focus on traditionally female-related topics, and their male counterparts focus on those things suited for traditionally male-oriented behaviors. The child's filtering mechanisms guide them to see and hear different things; and to see and hear the same things differently.

From our earliest history as hunters and gatherers, up through the 19th and 20th centuries and the Industrial Revolution, physical strength and endurance were the main attributes that governed judgments about productivity and roles. For the longest time, those traditional perceptions and role definitions have held true to form. Those perceptions also carried over into other beliefs.

If women are physically unable to perform the tasks required to work, it was believed, it only stands to reason that the woman's place is in the home, producing and taking care of babies. That belief carried with it a correlating belief: Then, why should women have a voice outside the home, such as being allowed to vote, or holding public office?

It has only been since the work environment began to change that those attitudes began to shift ... to a point.

With innovations such as the cotton gin and the sewing machine, and the emergence of the garment industry and other industrial innovations, attitudes began to soften, though maybe not as fast for men as for women. The perceptions went something like this ... OK, so maybe there are some limited areas where women could perform certain activities, such as sewing fabrics or cleaning factory floors. It is no coincidence that those changes in the workplace were also accompanied by changes in women's attitudes and beliefs toward social issues such as women's suffrage, for example.

Then, World Wars I and II enabled an even bigger leap for women in the workplace, at least in the United States. As men marched off to war, the women conveniently, and quite ably, took their places in the factories, producing everything from tanks to bombers. Though those roles lasted only as long as the war lasted, the dye had been cast. Women could indeed perform in the workplace, even in non-traditional roles. That set the stage for changing the perceptions of the two genders in many respects.

While many women went back into the home, to begin producing and raising their Baby-Boomer children, others continued to make their mark in the workplace, and in society. From Eleanor Roosevelt, to Rosie the Riveter, to the creation of the U.S. Women's Army Corp, to the creation of the All-American Girls Professional Baseball League, changes abounded, as did the perceptions.

And today, as the agricultural and manufacturing economies–both of which had relied on physical strength and stamina–have given way to the more knowledge-based, information economy, the roles of women have reached new heights.

And, What About in the Workplace?

So, here we are in the 21st century, experiencing the most significant innovations, with the most diverse workforce in our history, yet some questions and perceptions remain. Are men stronger leaders than their female counterparts? Are women too emotional to make tough decisions? Are women capable of running major corporations ... or countries?

How do we shape our beliefs around those gender-based questions? The answers to these types of questions have been borne out, both by scientific studies and actual occurrences, but old perceptions tend to hang around.

Now, before we proceed further, we must pause ... .

Hopefully, thus far in this segment, we have successfully tiptoed around the delicate and often contentious issues of gender bias, gender equality, equal pay, etc. Those are all valid discussions, but we will leave those for other forums. Our focus in this segment is about perception ... how perceptions differ between males and females and how those variances might contribute to changes in behavior, especially in this dynamic era.

So far, this is what we know:

- *We know the percentage of women in the workplace is increasing.*

- *We know the rate of women occupying key roles in the workplace is on the rise.*

- *We know that women are being hired into leadership roles, including as CEOs, at increasing rates.*

- *And, we also know women are bringing different perceptions into the workplace, and those different perceptions lead to different behaviors, different aspirations.*

In what is described as the largest comprehensive study of women in the workplace, McKinsey & Company and LeanIn. org conducted a study they called *Women in the Workplace 2018*.

Among the highlights of the study, we learn that women of different ethnicities agreed their agenda is to (1) deliver value to their company, and (2) serve as a role model for others. Their aspiration, the study tells us, is more about performing quality work versus climbing the corporate ladder (Krivkovich & Nadeau).

While women tend to be less motivated than their male counterparts to get promoted, women are very motivated to be treated equally. And they tend to be increasingly assertive in demanding that equal treatment. While men might perceive that assertive behavior as the pursuit of a promotion, women would say, according to the study, it's simply about having equal access and an equal voice.

This speaks to another aspiration which women tend to pursue with more vigor and enthusiasm than their male counterparts … *the opportunity to influence the culture of my workplace.* There tends to be a greater desire for their success to serve as a role model for others, and being recognized for their achievements is a means of modeling their behaviors for others, as much as it has to do with personal advancement.

The findings from the McKinsey/LeadIn.org study are consistent with those outlined in the book by authors Sophie Hahn and Anne Litwin titled *Managing in the Age of Change: Essential Skills to Manage Today's Workforce.* In their publication, the authors cite similar views that women bring into the workplace that may differ from males, citing behavioral examples ranging from problem-solving, conflict management and organizational structure.

According to the authors, women perceive that individual work styles should be collaborative, where everyone works as part of a whole, whereas men tend to believe work should be completed more independently with less assistance from others.

The perceptual differences between the genders, many would suggest, originate in the womb, and are then further shaped by our cultures, and in many instances, re-enforced in the workplace. Those perceptions, historians will tell us, have largely been established by a male voice. Enabled by evolution and a more knowledge-based economy, females are gaining strides and have begun to demand an equal voice.

Our perceptions should not shift to become female-centric, no more than male-centric, they say, but balanced.

Conclusion

Of the various elements we have analyzed, perhaps none are as well-documented as the perceptions related to gender. Perhaps, none are as potentially contentious and fraught with landmines. The themes are consistent and pervasive across geographical boundaries and cultures:

- *Males and females are genetically wired differently.*
- *Those genetic differences are the spawning ground for a rich history of beliefs and stereotypes of how males and females are taught to view each other.*
- *Those beliefs have historically been slanted towards and by a male-oriented society.*
- *Women are emerging to carve out a different view of themselves, both in society and in the workplace.*
- *Consequently, our perceptions, both of ourselves and the opposite gender, are evolving!*

The key take-away? Just as in our segment on culture, we caution, before you judge the behavior, understand the reason.

Our beliefs about gender roles began in the earliest stages of our lives, and have guided us through our educations and into the workplace. From the United States to the deepest corners of Africa and South America, the differences vary by culture, but the results have been largely the same.

Nowhere have those beliefs been more evident than in the workplace, ironically the area where women have made some of their most dramatic strides toward equality. From the statistical rise of women in the workplace to the many studies that have demonstrated equal, and in some cases, superior cognitive abilities and leadership attributes.

In the final analysis, women are encouraged to continue pushing the envelope to voice their opinions, pursue more leadership roles, more entrepreneurial ventures and more executive presence in the world of business and politics. Men, on the other hand, are encouraged to break free of the traditional stereotypes about women that have existed for centuries, and look to new ideas and innovations with their female counterparts.

Mahatma Gandhi once told his followers, when contemplating candidates for the Prime Minister role for the newly independent India, "Ideas and inspiration come in many forms, shapes and sizes, male and female." He told of how he frequently consulted his wife on various issues he engaged in and spoke of. He reminds us that we all see through a different lens.

Chapter Four
Perception and Intelligence

The more you know, the more you realize you don't know.

Aristotle

Introduction

This was a tough one. Our challenge was to examine how our perceptions impact our intelligence. What we encountered as we pursued that question, however, was an overwhelming number of scientific studies, nuances and distinctions between being "intelligent," being "smart" and being "knowledgeable."

There is the question of how our perceptions impact our intelligence, then there is the question of our perceptual quotient, or PQ, both of which we will address.

As far as how our perceptions impact our intelligence, the body of work on the subject is significant, but we're hesitant to try to squeeze it all into this segment. There's an expression that says, "Don't tell everything you know; just tell what they need to know." From the very beginning, our objective has been to provide a practical application on the various aspects of perception, as opposed to writing a scientific treatise on the subject. So, we decided, less is more.

It is for that reason that we minimized our focus on the scientific aspects of intelligence, i.e., the brain, IQ, or other DNA-related factors; instead, we placed our emphasis on the more pragmatic perceptual aspects of "what does this mean for me?"

With that objective as our guide for the purposes of this discussion, when we write of intelligence, we are also writing about being smart and knowledgeable. We even went so far as to apply our own, very unscientific definition of the word:

Intelligence (n): *What we know and how we apply what we know.*

Now, while the behavioral scientists in our audience may want to quibble with our approach (and our definition), our goal is to distill what is a very complex topic into practical and applicable concepts. With all of that said, we come to the central question: "How do our perceptions shape our intelligence, i.e., what we know and how we apply what we know?"

Even with our simplified approach, the answers are still somewhat complicated, (1) because there are different forms of intelligence (more about that later); (2) because our intelligence is developed and evolves in different ways; (3) because our perceptions continue to evolve and change; and (4) because different cultures perceive intelligence in different ways.

Then, there is the whole notion of "Perceptual Intelligence."

Let's take those one at a time, beginning with the different forms of intelligence.

Fluid vs. Crystalized Intelligence

In the 1960s, a British psychologist named Raymond Cattell put forth the proposition that intelligence takes two distinct forms. The first is our foundational intelligence. That, Cattell said, equates to our base level knowledge, generally formed through our early learnings and experiences. We learned 2 + 2 = 4. We learned our ABCs. We learned that dogs can bite, and bees can sting. That foundational intelligence, which relies heavily on our experiences of past knowledge or learnings, is what Cattell referred to as "crystalized" intelligence (Brown, 2016).

He then introduced a second type of intelligence that equates to our ability to grasp new learnings or new experiences, which he referred to as "fluid" intelligence. That is the form of intelligence that makes us adept at grasping new experiences, new concepts, and solving new problems. Cattell, along with one of his former students, John Horn, went on to research the subject further and write a series of publications on fluid versus crystallized intelligence. It was their work which changed a number of those earlier beliefs on the subject.

Their work was also instrumental in destroying another earlier theory, that intelligence could not be developed. That belief, which we will discuss later in this chapter, was dramatically changed when they conducted a variety of studies which demonstrated that fluid intelligence could indeed be developed.

Those studies put the subject of intelligence in a brand-new light.

Types of Intelligence

To take the analysis of intelligence one step further, in the 1980s, another psychologist, Howard Gardner, led a series of studies to examine other elements of our intellect. He studied things such as talents and special abilities, which were traditionally viewed only as ancillary traits to intelligence. He determined those traits were not ancillary at all but were different forms of intelligence.

Just because someone is not good at math, Gardner concluded, it does not mean they are not intelligent (Cherry, 2019). Intelligence comes in different forms or specialties, he said, and in 1983, he wrote of nine different types of intelligence (*Edutopia*, 2013):

1. Naturalist Intelligence
2. Musical Intelligence
3. Logical-mathematical Intelligence
4. Existential Intelligence
5. Interpersonal Intelligence
6. Bodily-kinesthetic Intelligence
7. Verbal-linguistic Intelligence
8. Intra-personal Intelligence
9. Visual-spatial Intelligence

The concept of intelligence was no longer binary, but now multi-dimensional. To further add to the topic's growing complexity, scientists also began to dissect the IQ test itself, to look at the true measure and behavioral meaning of intelligence. If one is regarded as being smart, what differentiates that person from one who is regarded as very smart?

Intelligence testing has become more refined, to look beyond the individual as a whole, to examine the multiple categories in which individuals can be measured. One can be viewed as "very smart" when it comes to mathematics or engineering-related issues, but not very smart at all when it comes to social skills or other parameters. In many cases, one's perception of another's intelligence is influenced by the mastery of concepts within a particular field or mastery of actions within a particular situation.

So, how are those multi-dimensional views of intelligence impacted by our perceptions? The answer to that question is roughly dependent on three factors:

1) *To what extent do you value being "intelligent?"* While you would think everyone values intelligence, believe it or not, some cultures and sub-sets of cultures don't place a particularly high value on being smart. Especially if the perception is one of being brainy, or smart but impractical.

2) *In which categories of intelligence do you perceive to have the greatest importance?* Athletes, for example, might have little concern for your math or engineering-related intelligence, but would place significant value on your bodily-kinesthetic intelligence. And,

3) *How motivated am I to cultivate that intelligence?* That, too, is dependent on multiple factors. For example, I am more motivated if my livelihood is hanging in the balance than if I'm simply curious to learn something new.

All of those factors are driven by our perceptions … from the perceptions of what we believe to be important, to what other people may think, to perceptions of what is expected of us. Despite what we are or are not born with, much of our intelligence, what we know and how we apply what we know, is indeed shaped by our perceptions.

Now to the issue of our "Perceptual Quotient" or PQ.

Dr. Brian Boxer Wachler is considered to be an expert in human perception. He is the medical director of the Boxer Wachler Vision Institute in Beverly Hills and a staff physician at Los Angeles's famed Cedars-Sinai Medical Center. He has written numerous books and articles on the subject. One of those is titled *Perceptual Intelligence: The Brain's Secret to Seeing Past Illusion, Misperception, and Self-Deception.* In today's vernacular, that would be "How do you tell real news from fake news?"

In his publication, he explores the brain's ability to interpret between reality or fantasy and how to separate the two. Boxer Wachler explores the concept of "cognitive dissonance," i.e., how our brain and our senses do not always match reality, and how fine-tuning our perceptions can improve our ability to lead and influence others.

Improving your PQ, the author says, elevates your game so you can have more of what you want in life; whether that is a better job, better relationships, better sex, more success, more happiness, etc.

OK, so improved perception leads to a better life. So, what

does all this have to do with plain old perception ... how we view the world around us?

Well, we also learned that different cultures conceptualize and measure components of intelligence in various ways. Some cultures value a person's ability to quickly process and respond to information. Other cultures may value one's ability to consult with members of the same culture who have more life experience in order to solve problems. Still, other cultures value creativity, formal education, and literacy as a basis of intelligence.

Essentially, how we view someone as being "smart" tends to differ depending on the culture in which we grew up. Whereas in some Western cultures, individuals who are fast talking, fast acting, or, "quick on their feet," could be perceived as being intelligent, other cultures may place a higher premium on being more thoughtful and deliberate in the way they process information.

Witold Lisowski, a native of Poland, was a participant in an international training and leadership conference. As the team exercises were conducted in English, Witold (pronounced *Vee-told*), who is naturally reserved and spoke limited English, was quiet and offered little input during most of the exercises. It would have been easy for other team members to perceive Witold as being somewhat slow, or "unintelligent."

During one of the more challenging exercises, the team reached a point where they were stumped by the geometric puzzle they had been given as a problem-solving challenge. They decided to take a break and come back in fifteen minutes, to perhaps have a fresh view of the challenge. Witold remained behind, continuing to study the various pieces of the puzzle scattered across the table. When the other members returned from their break, Witold had singlehandedly completed the puzzle.

The least vocal and least engaging team member–or the "unintelligent" member of the group–had brought his team high honors in the highly competitive event. In other words, what's in here (pointing to the head), may not always be evident by what comes out here (pointing to the mouth).

Intelligence, like so many other ingredients necessary to achieve success in life, is necessary but not sufficient. Everyone knows a brilliant kid who failed school, or someone with mediocre smarts who made up for it with hard work, so scientists are looking at factors other than intelligence that help some students do better than others, or make some leaders more successful than others.

One of those is perceptual abilities. "One who can discern cultural and other subtleties," says Sophie von Stumm of the University of Edinburgh in the UK, "can go far beyond where their book smarts will take them, especially in this world of increased globalism."

Conclusion

The question, "What do we know and how do we apply what we know?" is not one which is answered simply. As we've outlined, there are many forms of intelligence, many factors that influence our intelligence, and many ways to develop our intelligence. There are even differences in how we view intelligence. So, invariably, the answers lead us into a wide array of "it depends" scenarios.

The question, "How is our intelligence affected by our perceptions?" however, can be answered much more clearly.

Let's start at the beginning.

Our perceptions are shaped by our culture and other factors which, in turn, shape our values, our personal interests, our curiosity and our motivation to learn. Without delving into the scientific aspects of the brain, IQ, or other DNA-related determinants, our perceptions, as a result, are one of the major drivers of intelligence.

Our perceptions influence what is important to us, what is interesting to us, what we want to learn more about, and what we want to develop further.

The English major in college whose mindset is focused solely on becoming a writer is probably rather uncurious about subjects like anatomy or astronomy, and hence, could be considered "unintelligent" in some areas, while intelligent in others.

The student who has been coached by his or her parents since childhood that education is essential to a good life might feel differently about those subjects, and as a result, would presumably be more motivated to become more "intelligent."

In each instance, it is our perceptions that shape our interests, our curiosity, and our *pursuit* of knowledge, and as a result, they shape how we develop our intelligence.

Chapter Five
Perception and Emotions

Emotions are not problems to be solved. They are signals to be interpreted.

Vironika Tugavela

Introduction

In a variety of forums, we have had discussions that included questions such as, "Do our perceptions influence how we feel? Do they shape our likes, our dislikes?" "What is the impact of our perceptions on things like being happy? Sad? Unhappy?"

At the root of those discussions is the fundamental question, "What is the connection between what we perceive, and how we feel?" "Do our perceptions influence our emotions?" And the inverse: "Do our emotions influence our perceptions?"

The answer on all counts is, "Absolutely!"

For example, what do you feel when you come upon a snake? Or when you're in a nice restaurant and see a couple at a nearby table displaying what you regard as inappropriate displays of affection? Or when you hear your name called as the one who received the big promotion? In short, the linkage between what we perceive and what we feel is undeniable, as is the inverse. The two sensations, researchers tell us, are psychologically joined at the hip.

From being swayed by advertisers who attempt to influence what we buy, to leaders who attempt to motivate us, to the visuals we see in magazines or publications, or the songs we hear, those perceptions are continually flowing directly into our emotions.

With that premise as the foundation, this chapter attempts to delve not only into the link between our perceptions and our emotions, but the impact that linkage has on our behaviors and our lives on a day-to-day basis.

Perceptions and Emotions

Do certain images or phrases conjure up emotions?

The Holocaust...

The "Me Too" movement...

Corporate lay-offs...

The coronavirus...

Scientists say, absolutely. Stephanie Pappas, senior writer for *Live Science* magazine, examined five examples of how our perceptions directly influence what we feel, and vice versa. Perceptions matter, she says. Happiness, sadness, anxiety and anger are all colored by the images we see or hear, leaving a subtle, but significant impact on how we feel.

For example, love makes things taste sweeter. Research published in January 2014 found that being in love actually makes food and drink seem sweeter. Researcher Kai Qin Chan, a doctoral candidate at Radboud University Nijmegen in the Netherlands, conducted a series of tests with subjects who defined themselves as either "in love" or not (Susskind, 2014).

The correlations were striking in finding those who described themselves as being in love described the same items as tasting significantly sweeter than those who professed "not" to be in love. The researchers concluded that the association between sweetness and love starts early, when babies learn to associate their parents' love with formula or breast milk (Pappas, 2014).

In a completely different realm, importance feels heavy. A heavier document, Pappas wrote, is generally perceived to be regarded as more important or more serious than one that is lighter. This phenomenon also works the other way. University of Cambridge psychologists told different subjects a book was full of either important information or fluff. When asked to judge the weight of the book, those who were told the document was full of important writing judged the document to be heavier than those that were told it was fluff.

Researchers also found the emotional sensation of feeling powerless also feels heavy. In a research project published in the February 2014 edition of the *Journal of Experimental Psychology,* subjects who described themselves as feeling "powerless" tended to perceive objects as being significantly heavier than those who expressed other emotions (Univ. of Cambridge). That effect, they showed, also carries over into one's motivation or actual performance. According to researcher Eun Hee Lee, those who described themselves as powerless tended not to overextend themselves, or try harder, feeling that they don't control the resources or the circumstances as a more powerful person might.

The perception of being lonely, researchers found, feels cold. Citing phrases such as, "I've been frozen out at work," "She greeted me with warmth," these studies found a direct link between that sensation and room temperature. Researchers asked volunteers to recall periods in their lives of either loneliness or acceptance. They were then asked to estimate the temperature in the room. Those who described a period of loneliness or despair estimated the room to be 4 degrees Fahrenheit colder, on average, than those who described feelings of acceptance. In a follow-up study, researchers found that people excluded from a game were more drawn to warm foods like soup, presumably trying to warm their bodies in compensation for the chill of loneliness (Susskind, et al).

Hearing phrases like "black and white" can make you more judgmental. That very phrase, or even images of black and white, tend to literally make people's judgments more black and white. From a study conducted in 2012, when given a moral dilemma printed with a black-and-white border, people were more likely to make a strong judgment of morality or immorality, versus when the border was gray or colorful (Christensen, et al). In those instances, the subjects were more likely to see both sides of the story.

In an article published in 2008 in *Nature Neuroscience,* authors Joshua M. Susskind and his colleagues discuss the linkage between fear and our perceptions. They explain how one of the functions of fear is to enhance our perceptions, including speeding up eye movements, and increasing nasal volume and air velocity during inspiration.

So, do these correlations vary by culture? According to Marianna Pogosyan, Ph.D., a lecturer in cultural psychology and a consultant specializing in the psychology of cross-cultural transitions, the answer is mixed.

The link between perceptions and emotions tends to be universal. But the way those emotions are expressed can vary by cultures. In an article she published with Jan Engelmann in the October 2016 edition of *Psychology Today* entitled "Emotion Perception Across Cultures," Pogosyan cites a series of studies of how our culture does have an impact on how we interpret facial expressions of emotion.

She describes how, at birth, our emotional expressions are universal, but as we grow, those expressions tend to be shaped by our cultural norms. Citing a series of studies between Japanese and American subjects, the author says, facial expressions and non-verbal behaviors tended to vary significantly between American and Japanese subjects. For example, she says, looking at the same images of expressions of happiness, sadness and surprise, the American subjects rated the emotions as being more intense than did their Japanese counterparts (Pogosyan & Engelmann, 2016).

Some cultures, she says, are simply more emotive or expressive about their emotions than others. She shares an example of how that can vary within certain cultures. Southerners within the United States, for example, can have the reputation as being more outgoing and, therefore, seem warmer than their counterparts in the northeastern part of the country.

Our cultures may not influence the link between our perceptions and our emotions, but very much influence how we express those emotions. To take that one step further, Pogosyan says, people are usually more accurate when judging facial expressions from their own culture than those from others. We tend to develop what she calls "cultural accents," which are non-verbal signatures specific to our cultures. Simply stated, some cultures are more expressive non-verbally than others, and those within those cultures learn to detect and replicate those behaviors.

This cross-cultural ability is what Pogosyan describes as "display rules," which are the cultural norms or influences that shape how we are expected to exhibit responses to certain stimuli. Culture-specific display rules are learned during childhood and tell us the appropriateness or inappropriateness of certain emotional displays.

These display rules were illustrated in a study in the 1970s when American and Japanese subjects were shown a stressful film, under two different sets of circumstances: one when they're alone, and one with an experimenter in the room with them.

Participants from both cultures produced similar facial expressions when watching the films alone. However, in the presence of the experimenter, the Japanese masked their negative emotions through smiles, whereas the American participants continued to display their negative emotions in front of the experimenter.

The conclusion was that the Japanese, just as do other cultures, have a tendency to conceal negative emotions in social settings in order to maintain group harmony; as opposed to Americans, who, because of their more individualistic nature, tend to be more expressive in public settings.

These "display rules" that we learn from our cultural upbringing, however, come with a caveat. Dr. Paul Ekman, professor emeritus at the University of California, San Francisco, and a renowned expert in detecting deception, explains that despite our cultural differences, there are certain expressions that we all share. Those "universal expressions," he says, are anger, fear, enjoyment, disgust, surprise and anguish. He further describes research in which blind individuals, who have no visual cues to guide them, exhibit the same facial expressions as anyone else when confronted with the same stimuli (Hamilton, n.d.).

What remains constant, however, despite these universal expressions, and the examples of cross-cultural differences in how we express our emotions, is the direct linkage between our emotions and our perceptions. Where our perceptions go, our emotions follow.

Happiness, for example, according to Dr. Michael A Schreiner, a psychologist located in Salt Lake City, UT who specializes in human behavior, is based completely on perception. Therefore, we can argue that the concept of happiness exists as a real construct.

No matter what your situation is, Schreiner says, it could be made better and it could be made worse, depending on what you focus on. He gives an example, saying, "Consider ten different events going on in your life right now. If seven of those events are positive, and three are negative, if your focus is on the three negative elements, even though you have many more positive occurrences to be thankful for, chances are you're not feeling happy. Conversely, if eight of the events are negative and only the remaining two are positive, if you focus on the positive ones, chances are much greater that you're feeling happy." Whatever your state of happiness or unhappiness may be, he says, is governed by your perceptions.

The people you regard as seemingly happy, he continues, go through difficult circumstances just like everyone else. They are confronted with their share of failures and disappointments. But they don't dwell on the negatives. They maintain their focus on the positives. When it's dark, they look for the stars. It is not their circumstances that make them happy or unhappy, according to Schreiner. It is how they view those circumstances.

This is not to suggest you ignore the negatives in your life, psychologists tell us. Just put them where they belong. They are not the defining existence of who you are. They are items that deserve your attention at the moment. Further, they are items to be resolved and then put in the "done" category, not to be reopened.

There is a tale of two Tibetan monks who were walking a wooded path one day. When they came upon a stream, there was a young woman who wanted to cross the stream but she was fearful of its currents. One of the monks picked the woman up and safely carried her across the stream. He put her down and the two monks then continued on their journey.

As they continued for another forty-five minutes or so, the second monk was silent, but visibly upset. In their tradition, touching a person of the opposite sex is a violation of one of their most sacred vows. The first monk could tell that his friend was affected by what had taken place, and while knowing the answer, he asked his colleague what was bothering him. The second monk replied, "You picked that woman up and carried her across the stream."

"I did," replied the first monk. "But I put her down some forty-five minutes ago, and you're still carrying her."

Happiness, frustration, sadness, jubilation … the entire gamut of human emotions are all governed by what we see, what we hear, what we read, and what we think. But primarily, they're governed by where we place our focus.

From the Black Knight in the Monty Python movie *In Search of the Holy Grail,* whose arms were severed in battle, and quipped, "It's only a flesh wound;" to Steve Jobs who returned to Apple Computer and turned his company into a juggernaut after being told the company was "virtually lifeless," the examples are plentiful. What you feel depends on what you see.

To take the syllogism one step further, what you see is a choice. Therefore, happiness is a choice!

Though she agrees with the concept, Silvia Garcia, CEO of Happiest Places to Work, warns us, "Don't confuse happiness with pleasure." She describes how, from the earliest days of the caveman and our survival instinct, our brain produces dopamine to aid in our escape from danger. It also, however, is the trigger that gives us a sense of reward in capturing prey, or surviving pressure situations (Hamilton, n.d.).

In today's world, that "rush" we get from capturing prey or surviving dangerous or pressure situations translates into the pursuit of "stuff." A promotion, a newer car, a larger bank account, a bigger house, etc. While those, she tells us, may be pleasurable, they are not the keys to happiness.

The counterbalance to the dopamine rush we get in our brain, she tells us, is the serotonin system. It is the hormone that makes us bond with people and feel part of something bigger than ourselves. It gives us our sense of belonging. It is the part of our brain that poses the questions, "Why do we work?" "Why do we live?" "What is my life's purpose?" "What is my passion?"

Those are the questions that lead us to happier, more fulfilling work, she says, and more fulfilling lives.

Perception and Emotional Intelligence

OK, so how does all this differ from the concept of emotional intelligence, or "EI?" That answer is a little different, but EI also is closely linked to perception. Some of the earliest studies of EI were conducted by a couple of psychologists named Peter Salovey and John D. Mayer. In their work, the two established that our emotions actually enhance our performance. This was in dramatic contrast to the previous belief of just the opposite; that our emotions tend to get in the way of critical performance issues requiring things like logical thought or unemotional reasoning.

In their article, "Emotional Intelligence," published in 1990, the two professors described emotional intelligence as:

"...the ability to monitor one's own and others' feelings and emotions, to discriminate among them and to use this information to guide one's thinking and actions."

This is where perception comes in.

According to the definition, being emotionally intelligent means, first, knowing thine own emotions; secondly, being able to detect (perceive) the emotions of others; and thirdly, then being responsive to those emotions or feelings. This is especially important when it comes to your performance in dealing with people, which most of us have to do.

If I'm having a bad day, I need to recognize that I'm having a bad day and, if possible, maybe not make any major decisions today. If you're having a bad day, I need to recognize that you're having a bad day, and incorporate that knowledge into how I interact with you. The perception of mine and other's emotions, studies tell us, is essential to being effective with people.

In an interview with former Campbell Soup CEO Douglas Conant, he talked about how the occasion of losing his job and working with an outplacement agency in his pending job search, completely turned around his leadership style and his career. He described how the agency greeted him with what he said were four magic words ... 'How can I help?'

Those four simple words, he says, became a cornerstone for how, in every job he's taken since, he learned the power of engaging disenfranchised employees. That simple question, Conant said, not only showed employees he cared about them, but made those employees want to work harder for him. Those four words, he said, were the catalyst that helped him increase profits when he became president of Nabisco, and do the same when he became the CEO at Campbell Soup.

In telling his story, Conant displayed all the attributes of EI. First, he recognized the impact people's emotions play in their day-to-day job performance; secondly, he showed an interest to ask how his employees were doing; and third, he was interested enough to listen to their answers!

Conclusion

Whether it be our own emotions and those of others; or, whether it be the ability to exhibit emotional intelligence in the way you interact with others, perception is the trigger for them all. What we believe, and what we see and hear impacts how we feel, and how we engage others. Inversely, what we feel has a similar impact on what and how we perceive.

Though there are additional factors in the equation, the cornerstone of being happy, Dr. Schreiner reminds us, is to 'guide your perceptions toward the things that make you happy and hang out with happy people.'

As we've discovered, our sensory perceptions are the launching pad of our emotions. They determine what feels good, what feels bad, indifferent, positive, negative, happy or sad. But be reminded, some of us, depending on where we're from, may display those emotions differently.

Try to guide your perceptions accordingly.

Chapter Six
Perception and Failure

> *Whether you believe you can or cannot do something, you are right.*
>
> *Henry Ford*

Introduction

How do you respond to your failures? Though every individual has their own unique reaction to those occasions in which they failed, their reactions tend to go in one of two directions ... Fight or flight ... Embrace it, or run from it.

Everywhere we turn, as we study the topic of perception and its relationship to leadership or success, we run into that question, "How do leaders perceive their failures, or more to the point, their fear of failure?" The answer seems to fall into that same, "half empty/half full" scenario.

Timothy Daniels and Anne Matthews were mid-level colleagues at a major technology firm and were given a very special assignment. The two were tasked to pay a visit to a high-profile customer who was very dissatisfied with a recent transaction with the firm. This was not the first time this customer had expressed unhappiness with the firm's performance. Timothy and Anne's task was to meet with the customer, let him vent, and then see what it would take to "make things right."

During the entire two-hour drive to the customer's site, Timothy was clearly anxious and apprehensive about the meeting. He was anticipating a very unpleasant meeting, saying to his colleague, "You know we're gonna get our @$$#$ handed to us on a silver platter, and you and I are the ones that are gonna take the brunt of it!"

As her colleague continued drive and share his dire expectations, Anne just listened.

When they arrived, it didn't take long for the pair to conclude Timothy was right. The customer didn't hold back. The product didn't work, he told them. The customer service was lousy. The delivery schedule lagged for more than a month. And the left hand didn't seem to know what the right was doing. And those were just the highlights of his dissatisfaction. The customer kept the two of them in their chairs for almost two hours, detailing a history of their company's poor performance, telling them he would never order from them again.

When Timothy finally got the chance to speak and ask him how their company could make things right, the customer's response was, "By getting out of my office, and taking your product that doesn't work with you!"

Whew! When they stopped for lunch on the drive back to the office, Timothy had nothing but a glass of water. He was emotionally spent from the grilling they had just received. He was further worried about how their boss was going to react when they would tell him they were unable to "make things right." Again, Anne appeared unfazed by the experience. If she was nervous or anxious, it didn't show. It was almost as if they had attended two different meetings.

As they were leaving the restaurant, Timothy said to her, "When we get back to the office, I'll let you tell the boss. I'm not even sure I would know what to tell him."

When they arrived back in the office, the two of them gathered in the conference room with the CEO and three other executives who were anxiously awaiting the update. They were already geared up to do what they had to do to make things right for the customer. They just didn't know what it would cost them. The CEO started the meeting by saying to the two, "Well … ?"

Timothy immediately motioned to his partner to respond. She began:

"We just had an extraordinary meeting. We learned more about ourselves as a company than I've learned in the five years I've been here. Here's the skinny … we lost a customer, but we gained some invaluable feedback which, if we take it, is going to make us an even stronger, more competitive company."

Timothy couldn't believe his ears. He just came from what he described as the worst customer meeting he had ever been in, and his colleague called it "extraordinary." As Anne continued, and the more he listened, the more he began to realize she was right, as did the executives. They were clearly disappointed by the loss of a customer, but were genuinely interested in the lessons learned as summarized by Anne. The CEO asked Anne to put those key points into a presentation and prepare to host one of the company's "lunch and learn" sessions.

Failure is simply the opportunity to begin again, this time, more intelligently. We celebrate our successes, but our growth comes from our failures.

Henry Ford

What is it that makes some of us perceive failure as bad, something to avoid at all costs, and others see it as good? Where some people try to shove their failures into the deepest recesses of their minds, others speak of them with relish, almost as if to embrace them.

What about you? How do you treat your past failures when preparing a biography, curriculum vitae, or job resume? Chances are they never see the light of day. Our fear seems to be that if we expose any of our past failings, we will diminish our value, or worse, present ourselves as a "failure."

Yet, our history is littered with successful leaders and entrepreneurs who cited multiple failures before eventually finding their success. From Abraham Lincoln, to Nelson Mandela, to Steve Jobs and Bill Gates, they each suffered multiple failures … enough to send most people packing. Yet, they managed to persevere right through the setbacks. What is the quality that enabled them to fight through their failures when most of us would have either given up and gone home, or chosen a different pursuit?

The answer, we found, does indeed fall into that half full/half empty characterization. But it gets portrayed in different ways. Let's begin with the scientific view.

Offensive or Defensive?

Dr. Theo Tsaousides is a neuropsychologist, assistant professor, and author of the book Brainblocks: Overcoming the Seven Hidden Barriers to Success. He says the fear of failure or atychiphobia–try to pronounce that one, its scientific name–

influences the type of goals you pursue, the kinds of strategies you use to achieve them, and the level of standards you set as indicators of success. He says, depending on your fear of failure, your actions are either offensive-minded, or defensive. In other words, your actions are either focused on achieving gains, or preventing losses.

Which are you?

For example, do you choose to work overtime because you don't want to be perceived as a slacker and risk getting fired? Or, do you work overtime to finish a new project in pursuit of a promotion?

Tsaousides cites several examples of how individuals with a high fear of failure tend to behave differently. They tend to avoid situations that might put them in the spotlight and be evaluated or judged. For example, he says,

- They may avoid making a sales pitch to an important client for fear of not closing the deal.
- They may set lower standards for themselves, even though they know they can do better, to avoid failure.
- Instead of making a face-to-face visit to close the deal, for fear of being rejected, they may simply choose to just make a phone call to avoid the possibility of being told "no."

In addition, he says, people with a fear of failure tend to intentionally create obstacles for themselves, which he calls self-handicapping, in the event they fail. For example, they may propose a sales call at a time when they know the client will be unavailable, or schedule a meeting knowing participants are unable to attend.

Dr. Tsaousides says, in the long run, this fear of failure

could lead to more serious problems with a person's physical and mental health, including feelings of fatigue, low energy and being emotionally drained. That, in turn, could lead to a general sense of dissatisfaction and self-destructive behaviors.

The fear of failure is perhaps the greatest inhibitor to pursuing difficult or challenging goals. It may keep you insulated from rejection or failings, but it can significantly limit what you choose to accomplish. In subtle, sometimes almost imperceptible ways, he says, our fear of failure can sabotage our careers, our relationships, or even our life goals.

If you fear that you may fall into this category, the first step in overcoming your fear of failure is getting a better understanding of what causes it and how it affects you. That begins with knowing which way you tend to lean … offensive or defensive.

In thinking about the answer to that question, let's look at some variations of how effective leaders, entrepreneurs and others lean.

Forward or Backward

John C. Maxwell is one of the most prolific authors and gurus on the subject of leadership, and of his many books on the subject, one we liked is *Failing Forward: Turning Mistakes into Stepping Stones to Success*. In it, Maxwell says the single ingredient that separates high achievers from average people is how they perceive and respond to failure.

Those who excel, he says, have the mindset that failure takes them a step closer to their ultimate objective. They embrace failure as a sign of progress. In some instances, he says, effective leaders almost get an adrenaline rush from failing, knowing that they're getting closer to their goal.

Where others may want to bury their failures in the sand, hoping to hide them from judgmental eyes, successful leaders almost want to trumpet their failures as badges of honor. According to Maxwell, the typical entrepreneur fails 3-4 times before they get their first taste of success. As they go through their failures, not only do they persevere, they gain momentum, knowing they're one step closer to the finish line. Successful entrepreneurs, he says, view failure as a friend, not an enemy. They also draw a big distinction between "failure" and "failing." Failing is just a temporary event. Failure is a characterization of an individual. Failing, Maxwell says, is merely a waystation to one's ultimate destination.

He reminds us that the essence of man is imperfection, so by definition, failing comes with the territory. Success is not the absence of failing. It is learning from your failings and changing your course. Those who refuse to embrace and learn from those mistakes, he says, wind up working for those who do.

In the end, Maxwell leaves us with a simple mantra, "Fail early, fail often, but always fail forward."

Reward or Punish

For most of us, our fear of failure can also stem from the possible outcome as a result. Somehow, we fear, we're going to suffer because of having failed. Somehow, we're going to be punished. Google, the search engine giant, after analyzing the many successes it experienced, actually began to reward failing.

Early in the company's creation, the company realized that some of their greatest innovations came from projects that were initially deemed failures. They came to conclude, in fact, that failure was the foundation of their competitive advantage as a company. As a result, they wanted to find a way to encourage people to fail, without fear of retribution. In 2012, they found their answer in what was launched as Project Aristotle.

The project examined the behaviors of 180 of their strongest teams to figure out why some excelled beyond others. The study revealed that the more successful teams created a much more intimate and humane environment, one built on respect and mutual trust. That atmosphere of trust, they found, allowed team members to openly challenge one another and express their failings without fear of consequence or ridicule.

"Mistakes are inherent in our business and essential to our company's creativity and innovation," said one of the researchers. "How we react to those mistakes either encourages or discourages project members to openly discuss them."

As a result of Project Aristotle, Google established a reward system for failures. Their belief was that by rewarding people to fail, it encouraged and incentivized them to take greater risks and pursue greater breakthroughs.

The company even took the idea one step further. They created Google X, which they described as their "moonshot factory," where employees can create and collaborate on the most truly outlandish and audacious ideas. "We want to create the expectation that all ideas can be worth exploring," the project creator said, "and that failures are simply learning opportunities that take us further toward realizing those ideas. In doing so, we want our employees to change their perception of failure and use it on their path to success. Failing is our enabler to achieve great things."

The result? Google remains one of the most successful and innovative companies of our era, and if they continue their focus on failing, they'll most likely continue to hold on to that title.

Confront or Avoid

As a young lawyer, Mahatma Gandhi traveled from India to South Africa when he was hired to handle a commercial dispute in that country on behalf of a local Indian trader. He had known of the country's practice of apartheid, but didn't realize how brutal or how denigrating the practice was until he experienced it firsthand. The legal dispute for which he was hired turned into a 21-year crusade in which he remained to fight the evil practice on behalf of all persons of color in the country.

In doing so, he quickly began to realize his biggest battles were not only with the South African government, but also with those same persons of color he hoped to help.

The government's practices had become so prevalent and so instilled in the country's black and Indian populations that they had settled into an acceptance of the practices which rendered them to be second-class citizens. Further, the government's brutal reactions toward anyone who challenged those practices left the population fearful. The consequences could result in loss of property, beatings, jail or even death.

It is here that Gandhi cultivated and preached his strategy known as *satyagraha* (truth-force). He led the campaign to oppose the oppressive practices through peaceful, non-violent protests. The locals not only feared that the strategy would fail, but also that violent repercussions could result.

The diminutive, mild-mannered lawyer, in preaching the strategy of *satyagraha* (truth-force) and non-violent protests, told the locals they must confront their fears, including the risk of violence, to confront the wrongs of the government.

"As long as we keep running from our fears," he told an audience of Indian leaders in the country, "they will keep chasing us, and they will keep winning. Success can only be found in confronting our fears."

"Which do you choose," he asked, "the truth and your dignity, or your fears?"

Velcro or Teflon

When hearing Velcro or Teflon, we think off these as two diametrically opposite creations; one creates the sensation of sticking to whatever it touches, while the other does just the opposite. Using that analogy, we learned from our study of the reticular activator in the brain that we have the ability to do both. So, our question is, which things do you allow to stick to you, and which things do you let slide off of you?

Consciously or subconsciously, we make choices about what sticks in our memory (Velcro), and what rolls off of us like water on a duck's back, as the expression goes (Teflon).

For example, in the earlier scenario, after Timothy and Anne met with the irate customer, what was Timothy's Velcro and what was Anne's? Conversely, what was their Teflon? It appeared to us that while Timothy's reticular activator was clinging to the scolding he heard from the customer, Anne's was clinging to something very different ... those valuable lessons.

That scolding probably stayed with Timothy into the night and long afterward. But to Anne, the scolding she heard was like Teflon. She had other, more meaningful things to cling to. What we remember and what we forget is a major factor in either contributing to or diminishing our fear of failure.

In an interview with *Golf Magazine,* Jack Nicklaus, the world-class golfer, was asked about his many victories, including those at the U.S. Open, the Masters and the British Open. Amazingly, Nicklaus was able to recount with a vivid memory each tournament and each shot on every hole. The interviewer then asked about tournaments he had lost, pointing out occasions when he hit bad shots in crucial moments. In multiple instances, Nicklaus replied, "I don't remember that."

Finally, the interviewer asked, "You mean to tell me that you remember the victories, but don't recall the defeats?"

Nicklaus replied, "Of course I remembered them then. At the time, I obsessed over them. But when the tournament was finished, I went to the driving range and stayed til I corrected my mistakes. Then I forgot them." The golfer explained, "You have to choose what you remember and what you forget."

Nicklaus, as do most successful entrepreneurs and leaders, are masters at the concepts of Velcro and Teflon. Their strategy is a variation on "love them and leave them." Theirs is what we call, "learn and leave." Embrace the failures, learn from the failures, then leave them behind.

Which is your Velcro? And, which is your Teflon? The confidence-building victories? Or the times you failed?

As we previously learned, the reticular activator of your brain is currently working non-stop, whether you know it or not. It is filing away your Velcro moments, and using its Teflon abilities to discard the others. You have the power to determine which is which.

Do you remember your failings and get a sinking feeling in your stomach that you'd like to forget? Or do you view them as another step toward your ultimate goal?

The choice is yours.

Conclusion

So, what have we learned here? Each of these scenarios takes a different slant on our perceptions about the fear of failure, but they all seem to have the same binary, half empty/half full nature to them. Run from failure, or embrace it! Offensive or defensive? Learn from it, or pretend it never happened. Velcro or Teflon.

Are your actions intended to prevent you from getting fired, or to seek a promotion? Do you voice your creative ideas at the risk of judgment or ridicule? Or, do you keep them to yourself? Do you hesitate to pursue new opportunities for fear of being rejected? Do you seek feedback from your boss to learn how you can be better? Or, do you shy away, because you fear what you might hear?

James E. Aarons, in his autobiographical book, *Fear of Failure,* reminds us that our typical response is to avoid that which is painful or uncomfortable. But growth, he says, is based on confronting what is uncomfortable.

There is an expression that architects use when renovating an old building, "If you can't hide it, feature it." If that ugly support beam standing in the middle of the room must remain for structural reasons, then figure out how to make it part of the architectural landscape.

The same applies to failure. As John Maxwell reminded us, given that man is fundamentally imperfect and failure comes with the territory, we may as well figure out how to use it and learn from it.

Chapter Seven
Perception is Your Reality

> *How could they see anything but the shadows if they were never allowed to move their heads?*
>
> *Plato*
> *'The Allegory of the Cave'*

S o, what have we learned in the first segment of our study of perception and what factors influence our perceptions? Given the uniqueness of our cultures, our human qualities, our spiritual beliefs or non-beliefs, and other factors all play a part in shaping our perceptions. In essence, we've not only learned the factors that drive and shape our perceptions, we've also learned that our perceptions are about as unique and individualized as we are as human beings. This has led us to slightly modify the well-worn phrase, *perception is reality,* to say that our perceptions are our *own version* of reality.

Up to now, to fully understand these various dynamics that shape our perceptions, we have looked to leading behavioral scientists, business leaders, academics and entrepreneurs. To put an exclamation point on the subject, however, we look not to the academics or the behaviorists, but to the classics. Philosophers and authors have written about this topic from the beginnings of our civilization. Whether we got the message or not, it appears they tried to teach us these same lessons centuries ago.

In a previously cited interview I conducted with best-selling author Tom Peters, our discussion on perception brought us to the topic of what he described as probably "the most famous psychological experiment," which is best known as the "missing gorilla" exercise.

In the book by the same title, researchers and authors Christopher Chabris and Daniel Simons showed their subjects a group of two teams arranged in a circle, each passing a basketball around. One group of team members wore black shirts and the other team wore white shirts. As the members of each team continued to playfully pass their basketball around to their teammates, the experimenters asked the subjects to count the number of passes the white team completed during the exercise.

As the approximately one-minute exercise was underway, a figure in a black gorilla suit casually injected himself into the circle as the teams nonchalantly continued passing their basketball.

In the subject's feverish efforts to concentrate on how many times the white team passed the basketball, they completely missed the presence of the gorilla being inserted into the exercise.

In their book, *The Invisible Gorilla,* the authors use a wide assortment of stories and counterintuitive scientific findings to reveal an important truth … what we perceive is not exactly what is. "We think we see ourselves and the world as they really are," the authors say. "But we're actually missing a whole lot."

Our Earliest Lessons on Perception Are Still True

Perhaps the great philosophers, Socrates, Plato and Aristotle, had differing views on many aspects of humankind. But they seemed to have the same conclusions on the topic of perception. They were, perhaps our earliest teachers on the subject.

In one of Plato's classic writings in *The Republic,* the "Allegory of the Cave," prisoners are chained and can only look at the walls of the cave while puppeteers bring many different objects and walk behind them. Through the fire's reflection on the cave's walls, each prisoner sees an illusion of the real object, thus perceiving things in very distinct ways.

Their illusions are their realities.

"Allegory of the Cave" explores the basic questions … Are we all perceiving reality in our own unique way? Is what we see around us real objects or shadows? Our perception injects meaning into the objects we see, and their true reality is as different as are the shadows from the real object.

Is the prisoners' inability to move their heads correlated to our inability to often perceive things from different angles, and are we constrained by our many experiences? Do our cultures, spiritual beliefs and biases, etc., foster our ability to see things differently? Or, are we constrained by those life experiences?

Those factors we've studied in Part I, which shape and guide our perceptions, have a dramatic impact on our abilities to view things differently. Abilities such as critical thinking, logic, imagination and creativity, etc.; items we will explore further in Part II.

In his study of perception in his writings on metaphysics, Aristotle views reality as "tangible and capable of observing through sensory mechanics, relying on critical explanation of how and why it functions beyond any dispute."

Ever the pragmatist, even if he acknowledges different interpretations of perceptions. "Again," the great philosopher wrote, "we do not regard any of the senses as wisdom, but giving us our most authoritative knowledge of particulars." In other words, what we know is not truth. It is simply what we know. Aristotle also warned us that "the least initial deviation from the truth is multiplied later a thousand fold."

Therefore, our perceptions are capable of consciously or subconsciously altering realities and their true meaning, depending on where we are in life, our outlook, and who we are as people. The result being that the number of realities match the number of humans on this earth. Thus, our realities are akin to those shadows on the wall in Plato's imaginary cave.

From the Philosophers to the Classics

It appears that the lessons of those great philosophers were passed on to the great literary masters of our time. Charles Dickens, for example, accentuated the point of multiple realities in the opening lines of his classic, *Tale of Two Cities.* "It was the best of times, and it was the worst of times." Depending on circumstances, life experiences, etc., for some it was the best, while for others, the worst. Tolstoy wrote in his opening of *Anna Karenina,* "All happy families are alike; each unhappy family is unhappy in its own way." Both authors illustrate how very diverse existences trigger very diverse realities.

Oscar Wilde echoed the same theme when he wrote, "We are all in the gutter, but some of us are looking at the stars." Then, there is the classic line by Edgar Allen Poe, giving his view of multiple realities and multiple perceptions when he wrote, "All that we see or seem is but a dream within a dream."

Though their works are as varied as the human condition, the message from the classic authors, as from the great philosophers, regarding perception is the same. They are all best summed up by C.S. Lewis: "What you see and hear depends a great deal on where you are standing, and also what sort of person you are."

Part II

How Our Perceptions Influence Our Behaviors

Chapter Eight
Perception and Collaboration

Individually, we are one drop. Together, we are an ocean.

Ryunosuke Satoro

Introduction

Collaboration, defined as the "mutual engagement of participants in a coordinated effort to solve a problem together," has become an essential ingredient in today's workplace. The days of sitting at a workstation or on an assembly line in isolation are fast being replaced by teams working together to solve complex problems. The Industrial Revolution and manufacturing economy are giving way to the digital age and information economy.

Collaboration has become a required skill set.

So, how do our perceptions enhance our ability to collaborate with others? Conversely, how do they hinder?

There is a long-held adage that we tend to work best with people we enjoy, and shy away from those we don't. Does that mean our perceptions and preconceived biases dictate when and with whom we'll collaborate, and not?

If our perceptions are the prism through which we perceive everything and judge everything and everybody, and collaboration has become one of the most critical skill sets in the information age, then we've got some work to do. How do we keep our perceptions in check to allow us to collaborate with others, under less than ideal conditions, or with less than ideal work colleagues?

The variables are endless … Does the project intrigue us, motivate us? Do we like our teammates? Do we like the project leader? Do I like the role I've been given? Will I be recognized for my work? Who is this project really benefiting?

And on and on … .

And that does not factor personalities into the equation. What if I'm one who is bottom-line focused and pay little attention to the feelings of others, and I'm working with someone whose focus is making sure everybody gets along? Clearly, we see things differently and focus on different things. How do those perceptions affect our ability to work together?

And then there's the environment, and our ages, and our genders, and every other factor that challenges our ability to play well with others.

Harvard professor Amy Edmondson conducted a TED talk on the Chilean mining disaster that occurred on August 5, 2010, when thirty-three miners were trapped a half mile below the surface of the earth under some of the hardest rock in the world. The conditions were filth, intense heat and enough food for 10 men for two days. There was no existing plan or technology to address the situation. No drilling technology invented was able to get through rock that hard and that deep, and they had no means to communicate with the miners. It was not even known if they were still alive.

Individuals from over forty organizations and seven countries were brought in to help rescue the miners, from geologists, to NASA scientists, to social workers.

Within 70 days, the team was able to rescue all 33 men.

"No one person, or even one leadership team, or one organization or agency, could have successfully innovated to solve this problem," Edmondson said.

None of the members knew each other. They were simply told that each of them were experts in their field. They didn't have the luxury of allowing any other perceptions about each other into their work. They had a problem to solve, and a very limited time to solve it, and under highly stressful conditions.

Chances are the diverse team that came together to rescue the miners had language barriers, cultural barriers, knowledge differences, and different beliefs about how to solve the problem. Chances are some probably didn't like or respect other members of the team.

At a time when teaming and collaboration as attributes have never been at more of a premium, how do individuals manage their own unique perceptions and successfully collaborate with others who have vastly different perceptions?

That is the question for this chapter.

How do we manage our perceptions in a way that enhances our ability to collaborate, and not hinder it? In short, how do we work effectively with others we may not even like?

Perception Can Kill Collaboration

Let's begin with one of the universal truths about the human condition: Perceptions are the foundations of our opinions; opinions are the foundation of our biases; and biases are an inhibitor to collaboration.

To take that one step further, our perceptions are unique to us as individuals, which means when two people get together, chances are opinions will differ. Throw culture into the mix, and you potentially have a recipe for conflict. With the creation of work teams, expand that number to five people (or ten), and then you've got a recipe for a train wreck.

This all comes at a time when working in teams and collaborating to solve problems is vital to the success of individuals and companies alike.

So, in many ways, this chapter can be subtitled, "How to keep your opinions and biases from derailing your ability to collaborate."

Me? Biases?

We are all (well, most all of us) convinced that we don't have biases. We're accepting of other cultures, other religions, other races, other opinions. That's like saying that we don't have opinions. Even the most bias-free individual has them, according to Andy Zynga, CEO of NineSigma, and they are sometimes almost imperceptible. In a *Harvard Business Review* article about the detrimental impact of bias on collaboration, Zynga said, "Implicit biases subtly influence how we see, respect, and work with others." In fact, our pre-disposal to prejudging others is a major stumbling block when it comes to collaborating, he says, "causing major issues within organizations because they breed stereotypes and can inhibit fair, equity-based workplaces."

He says that even though biases can be detrimental to teamwork and collaboration, teams can actually breed biases. He provides several examples of how some biases can actually thrive on teamwork, such as,

- *The Groupthink or Bandwagon Effect – When an individual's thinking can be swayed by the power or consensus of the group that can inhibit an individual from voicing a different opinion.*

Or,

- *The Blindspot Bias – When we are blinded by our own pre-conditioned thinking.*

Or,

- *The Confirmation Bias – When we seek out and latch on to only those opinions or data that support our existing view.*

In his article, Zynga offers many other ways that our biases, however subtle they may be, are lingering around teams, just waiting to influence our thinking. It appears the first step in not allowing our perceptions to inhibit our ability to collaborate is recognizing the subtlety and power of our biases and not falling victim to them.

So, how do you overcome them? To answer that question, let's look at an area of the globe that is known for effective teaming and collaboration.

Paul Keijzer, a business leader and HR professional, is the CEO and managing partner of Engage Consulting. With a focus on working with teams in Asia markets, he cites the Japanese as a culture that stresses teaming and collaboration, perhaps more than any other.

When asked about ways to maximize teamwork, especially in diverse environments, he says the starting point is being convinced that a team with diversity will better achieve your end result. If you're not convinced of that, he says, everything from there is an uphill battle.

Secondly, he says, answer the question: *Why do I want to work with this individual or this team?* If you can't answer that question, that too will make life difficult. Finding and reminding yourself of the answer to that question minimizes the potential for conflict.

Third, he says, get to know each other. People are much more willing to help people they know.

He also cites establishing "rules of engagement" as being a critical element. How will you resolve conflict? How will you introduce ideas, solutions, or other forms of input? With rules of engagement in place, he offers another counter-intuitive suggestion ... embrace conflict. That assumes the rules of engagement specify constructive conflict, as opposed to personal attacks. The ultimate outcome of constructive conflict, he says, is teams that work more closely, more effectively with each other.

Finally, Keijzer says, have fun. "We've all will worked with people we don't necessarily want as friends," he says. "But to be a successful leadership team, you have to reach a point where you can respect where each of you is coming from and at least enjoy each other's company in the workplace."

Erin Meyer offers another suggestion for culturally diverse teams. Meyer is a professor of Organizational Behavior at INSEAD, a graduate business school with campuses in Europe, Asia, and the Middle East. She is also the program director of Managing Global Virtual Teams and Management Skills for International Business, and the author of *The Culture Map: Breaking Through the Invisible Boundaries of Global Business*.

She says simply, pay attention and adapt to the culture! She tells of how, in some cultures, the boss is revered and accepted as the sole authority, while in others, the boss is viewed as being more of a facilitator than an authority figure.

She said the lesson was brought home to her when teaching a group of Heineken executives. Heineken, of course, is a Dutch brewing company, which she stereotypically thought would be earmarked by a lot of tall, blonde Dutch people. In 2010, Heineken purchased a big operation in Monterrey, Mexico, and now a large number of head-office employees come from northern Mexico.

Among them is Carlos Gomez, who described his experiences since moving to Amsterdam a year earlier. "It is absolutely incredible to manage Dutch people and nothing like my experience leading Mexican teams," Gomez said, "because, from my experience, the Dutch do not care at all who is the boss in the room."

She tells of another instance in which one her INSEAD colleagues, Professor André Laurent, polled hundreds of managers, asking: "Is it important for a manager to have the answers to questions that subordinates may raise about their work?" While 46 percent of the Japanese sample claimed it was very important for the boss to have most of the answers, only 7 percent of Swedes thought the same way.

During a research project Meyer conducted with colleague Elsie Shen, she told of an answer she was given by a Chinese diplomat to the same question. "In China, the boss is always right," he said, "and even when the boss is very wrong, he is still right."

How we treat authority is largely a function of the culture in which we were raised, and goes a long way in shaping the way we find answers to problems. We either collaborate with colleagues, or we look to the boss. For someone such as Gomez, who learned to lead in a culture where deference to authority is relatively high, it can be both confusing and challenging to lead a team where the boss is seen as just another member of the team. Knowing which culture is which is crucial. You may be insulting teammates and frustrating yourself at the same time.

Debbie Narver, a Cross Cultural Leadership Specialist located in British Columbia, Canada, offers yet another recommendation for cross-cultural teams. In addition to the necessities of setting clear expectations for performance, and allowing plenty of downtime for the individuals to decompress from the stress of working in new teams, she advises teams to informally educate one another on their cultures. They can create forums for cultural training programs, or ways the various team members can learn more about each other's culture.

A large multi-national firm conducted two-week leadership programs for their worldwide teams, consisting of some 40+ participants from Latin America, the U.S., Africa, Asia and Europe. The participants were organized into teams consisting of representatives from each geographic area and would compete to solve various leadership challenges.

But each evening, when the participants would gather for the usual happy hour, a different geographic area would host a Culture Night in which the participants from that geography teamed up to present an informal and lighthearted program designed to educate the other participants on the nuances and idiosyncrasies of their culture. These Culture Nights consistently ranked as the highlight of each group.

Erica Dhawan is another individual we found who stresses

the importance of collaboration, in what she calls "connectional intelligence." In our interview, the founder and CEO of Cotential and author of the book, *Get Big Things Done: The Power of Connectional Intelligence,* described collaboration, or "community" as one of the "Five C's" that are essential to getting things done. (The others being curiosity, combination, combustion and courage).

In her book, she describes how effective teams have different types of "connectors," a term she borrowed from Malcolm Gladwell. There are the thinkers, the enablers and the executers. All, she says, are effective at fostering teamwork and leveraging the collaborative power of the team.

Even technology companies are now getting into the multi-cultural and multi-national elements of collaboration. Slack.com provides a technology platform designed to facilitate collaboration across cultures. The firm has conducted significant research on the subject and has found that both employees and employers alike consistently cite collaboration as being critical to innovation and boosting employee morale.

Another technology company called InnoCentive allows individuals who are not even employees to collaborate with companies. InnoCentive's web-based platform allows companies to post their unsolved problems or unmet needs out to the Internet, and anyone, internal or external to the company, can submit proposed solutions in exchange for cash awards.

The value of collaboration across cultures is recognized as being essential to the success of both companies and individuals, and now technology and organizations are enabling all to foster and cultivate that key attribute.

OK, but what if it's not the culture? What if it's the individual that is impeding my efforts to collaborate? What if I simply can't get along with that individual?

We all confront this situation at various points in our careers. And after looking long and hard for some magic potion or silver bullet to solve this dilemma, unfortunately, we found there is none. The answer, instead, seems to boil down to simply having to work harder. Back to those pesky, universal truths about human behavior; it's just not as easy to work with people we don't like as it is to work with people we do. And if we had a choice in the matter, we'd probably choose not to work with them. But, in the work setting, we're bound to occasionally be teamed up with someone we simply don't care that much about. So, in those cases, what do we do?

Mark Nevins is an executive advisor, consultant, and coach who works with individuals, teams, and organizations to help them perform more effectively, efficiently, and profitably. He recently authored an article in the *Harvard Business Review* titled, "How to Collaborate with People You Don't Like." He boils the answer to that question down to these basic tenets, knowing that no one wants to hear them, but also knowing it has to be done:

#1 – Work harder to understand the other person's perspective. As difficult as it may seem, he says, try to find that person's point of view and what's motivating their behavior.

#2 – Ask questions. Seek to verify their viewpoint, and have them talk about it.

#3 – Try to embrace their perspective. Acknowledge their perspective, which does not mean you agree with it. People know that others may not agree with them, but they want to be acknowledged.

#4 – Be a problem solver, not a critic. Explore ways their cryptic issues may be solved, or even put aside for the sake of the project.

Nevins goes on to also implore individuals to revert to their emotional intelligence, which is to be aware of your own emotions, as well as the emotions of others. Explore how other individuals may be perceiving you. After all (gulp), you could be contributing to the problem as well. Further, he reminds us to keep the issue focused on the task at hand, not on personal issues or dislikes.

Conclusion

Our perceptions can lead us into all sorts of roadblocks that can impede our ability to collaborate, which has emerged to be one of our most critical skill sets in this age of the information economy. From cultures we don't understand, to concepts we don't agree with, to people we don't like, there can be more reasons *not* to collaborate than to collaborate.

Whether we view our work to be inspiring, or sheer drudgery; whether we view our boss to be knowledgeable or clueless; whether we view our co-workers to be supportive or career threatening; our work and our ability to collaborate with others can be derailed by our perceptions.

Success in our jobs requires us to expand our perceptions. From digging deeper to understand another's culture that is different from our own, to asking more questions to learn why a co-worker can be so annoying, managing our perceptions will ultimately govern how well we are able to engage and influence others.

"Love me or hate me," Steve Jobs once told his Apple co-workers, "our job has nothing to do with how you feel about me. It has to do with being the most innovative company in the world."

Chapter Nine
Perception and Innovation or Creativity

Embrace your reality ... then change it.

Theodore Roosevelt

Introduction

This is where the fun really begins!

Thus far, much of our analysis has been about how perceptions create biases and predisposed thinking, and how it has the potential to influence our decision-making, engagement and collaboration. We were warned in many of those scenarios about how our perceptions are critical, but are capable of getting in our way because of those behaviors.

The relationship between our perceptions and our creativity appears to be no different. Our perceptions can be creativity's best friend or its worst enemy.

The first thing we learned is that there is an almost exact correlation between our perceptual experiences and our creativity. Want to be more creative, they say? Do more, travel more, experience more, live more. Take a different route to go to work. The more we see, hear and experience, the more creative we are.

The second thing, they tell us, is to be more comfortable and accepting of ourselves. Studies examine how, from childhood, we're conditioned to seek approval and gain affirmation and acceptance from others. From birth, beginning with our parents and other adults, to classmates, to teachers, to the opposite sex, we are trained to seek approval from others. That strong urge to comply and conform, studies have shown, can have an adverse effect on our creativity.

The forces of conformity, we have learned, are powerful. From our parents to our culture, they weigh heavily against creativity. Sir Ken Robinson reminded us in his TED Talk of how our education systems were designed in the 19th-century to accommodate the needs of the Industrial Revolution. A system that preaches rote memorization and conformity is hardly what is needed in the 21st-century information economy.

To examine the impact our educational system is having on the effects of creativity and innovation, Professor George Land created an assessment as part of his work with NASA to test for creativity. In the process, he studied children to see how their levels changed throughout time. At the age of five, 98% of children were tested to be creative geniuses. By the age of ten, that number had fallen to 30%. By age fifteen, it dropped down to 12%. And by age thirty-one, only 2% of the subjects tested to be considered creative geniuses.

The creative ones among us are not necessarily the ones who have scored the highest on standardized tests. Individuals, for example, are now using different pronouns on their social media profiles (they/them/theirs or she/her/hers etc.). This opens up a whole new dimension and set of challenges for employers and human resource professionals.

Think about the most creative individuals you know, and you'll find a little bit of maverick in them … maybe a lot of maverick! You'll also probably find them to be comfortable in their own skin and seemingly unconcerned about what others may think. That self-acceptance, behavioral scientists tell us, frees them up to experiment and be different, be unconventional, and hence, more creative.

The Art of Seeing Things Differently

In the 1989 movie, *Dead Poet's Society,* Robin Williams portrayed a high school English teacher at a small private school in Vermont who inspired his students through a variety of unorthodox methods, including having the students stand on top of their desks to "look at life in a different way." To make life extraordinary, he told his students, "To make a difference, you must see things differently."

In 1963, professional golfer Jack Nicklaus was enroute to the first of his six Masters Tournament championships. On the pivotal 12th hole, the famous golfer stood behind the fifteen-foot putt to get an accurate line on the break of the ball to the hole. Known for his precision, Nicklaus told his caddie he calculated the putt would break about four-and-a-half inches to the right.

His caddie had examined the putt from a completely different angle … from a side view. "Come over here and look at it from here," the caddie suggested to Nicklaus. "I don't think it breaks that much." Nicklaus was also known for viewing his putts from every angle, so he looked as his caddie suggested.

After studying the different angle for a few seconds, he looked at his caddie and said, "You're right. From this angle, it looks like it only breaks about three inches. Good call!"

Having adjusted his calculation as per his caddie's input,

Nicklaus sank the putt, and went on to win his first Masters Tournament.

While some of us can be virtually blinded to new concepts, new thoughts or different perspectives because of our cultural or spiritual filters, others are more comfortable putting those things aside to let the possibilities flow. Allowing ourselves to suspend our judgments, or our belief systems, seems to be a major prerequisite to creativity.

After all, weren't Orville and Wilbur Wright told that man is not meant to fly? Crazy mavericks!

The Paradox of Corporate Innovation

In 2013, the phenomenon of technical innovations was beginning to accelerate at an unprecedented rate. New innovations in areas such as cloud computing, robotics, artificial intelligence, micro-technologies, and others were hitting the market at a rate faster than companies could absorb them. The ability for companies to innovate was moving from a "nice to have" to a "must have" just to survive.

According to a 2013 study conducted by the consulting firm Accenture titled "Why Low Risk Innovation is Costly," 93% of global CEOs believe their organization's success depends on its ability to innovate. Yet, the study found that only 14% of organizations are satisfied with their innovation efforts.

This is supported by what Francesca Gino, Harvard Business Professor, told us in Chapter 11 on Perception and Curiosity. Many of those same leaders say they value curiosity in their workforce, but her research findings suggest just the opposite.

She says what leaders really value is order and control. So, why the discrepancy? Part of the answer was right in front of us.

Physical vs. Virtual

Rheinhold Hoffman was a client engagement manager for a machine manufacturing company in Germany. They produced large industrial machines for manufacturers, warehouses and other commercial entities. His company was preparing a bid for a major automotive company in Germany, and he was leading the team's proposal preparation.

The customer was in the market for an improved assembly line system, but with a twist. They had recently been cited by their government for environmental violations in their manufacturing process. So they were in the market for a customized machine to perform the same functions as their existing equipment, but at a significant reduction in the production of toxic gases.

Rheinhold's company knew they were not the leading supplier in this horse race, and would have to offer something that worked, would be competitively priced, and would stand out against the competition. They produced a prototype for the proposed product, but it would be too large and bulky to demonstrate to the selection committee. The obvious alternative was to present a video presentation, but Reinhold lobbied to do something a little more "hands on."

On the day of the presentation, four companies arrived to present their proposed solution. Each of the first three presented high-quality video presentations, and the eleven members that comprised the selection committee seemed impressed with each.

When it was time for Reinhold's team to present, they asked for a brief intermission to allow them to set up their presentation.

When the members of the committee returned to the auditorium, they found their chairs rearranged around a covered table which appeared to house a modeled solution of some sort. As Reinhold began his presentation, he explained the functionality and benefits of his team's proposed solution and then removed the cover from the mock-up to find a design made of ... colored Lego blocks.

He invited the team to stand and get closer as he guided them through the Lego block model. What began as a presentation turned into an active participant-based discussion, with members of the selection committee physically touching and maneuvering different blocks as they asked their questions. The entire committee found themselves in a hands-on simulation of the proposed solution, based on a simulation made of Lego blocks.

Based on their experience with the Lego blocks, the selection committee agreed to visit the company's headquarters to examine the prototype. Rheinhold's team won the bid.

In their write-up of their rationale for selecting the winning team, five members of the committee specifically mentioned the value of their Lego experience in their analysis.

The physical act of touching and manipulating the proposed solution, appeared to outweigh the more sophisticated, "slicker" video solutions.

What we've learned may seem intuitively obvious to many ... in a world that is becoming increasingly virtual, the ability to touch and feel generally outweighs what we can only see.

There are several studies which appear to illustrate the same point.

Terri L. Griffith is Professor of Management at Santa Clara University in California, and John E. Sawyer is the founder and Director of the Graduate Program in Organizational Effectiveness, Development, and Change at the University of Delaware. The two collaborated on a project to examine how changing perceptions can trigger innovation.

In an article they published in the November 2008 edition of the *Ivey Business Journal,* a publication that studies innovation in the workplace, the two write of the marvels of and impact of today's emerging technologies. They cite examples, such our abilities to simulate earthquakes with great precision, other forms of virtual reality, and the many other examples of 21st century innovations.

But, they tell us in the article titled "Changing Perceptions and Triggering Innovation," these technologies are also relatively abstract. Our innovations, they say, are best when our perceptions can be stimulated in a more concrete world, as opposed to the virtual world.

One of the most dramatic examples the authors cite of how tangible objects are more effective in spurring our innovation is the tense drama that unfolded on Apollo 13.

"Houston, we have a problem." When astronauts Jim Lovell, Jack Swigert, and Fred Hayes were suspended helplessly in space due to an electrical explosion, their fellow astronauts on the ground had to figure out how to solve the problem. When the engineers were exploring solutions from their flight simulators, the astronauts on the ground eventually fabricated a connection using a sock, plastic bag, pressure suit hose, cardboard manual cover, and duct tape. With that jury-rigged concoction, they were then able to communicate the solution to their colleagues lingering in space.

The authors cite several other examples, such as "cloud" computing, of how technology is taking us deeper into the virtual world, and explaining, "The more concrete the trigger, the more likely a new perspective will be engaged, and with it, the chance for innovation."

> *It is not the strongest of the species that survive, nor the most intelligent, but the one most responsive to change.*
>
> *Charles Darwin*

Forget What You Know...

In previous chapters, we've learned how our perceptions can get in the way. We come into situations with long-held beliefs in biases that can either obscure or render us blind to new experiences.

We learned of instances where our deep-seated cultural or spiritual beliefs can inhibit or certainly influence such essential behaviors as critical thinking or collaboration. It turns out our perceptions can have the same effect on our ability to innovate.

Robert I. Sutton, professor of management science at Stanford University, has spent much of his academic career exploring the intersection between psychology and leadership. When it comes to innovation, he tells us that while acculturation is essential to our integration into society, it is sometimes not our best friend when it comes time to innovate. He said, "To build a company where innovation is a way of life, rather than a rare accident that can't be explained or replicated, people need to discard their deeply ingrained beliefs. You have to challenge how the world is perceived in order to trigger innovation."

In one of the many books he has authored on the subject, *Good Boss, Bad Boss: How to Learn from the Best,* Sutton challenges his readers to put their perceptions to the test. He says, "Listen to those under your supervision. *Really listen.* Don't act as if you're listening and let it go in one ear and out the other. Faking it is worse than not doing it at all."

Citing multiple studies, Sutton says when people are put in positions of power, they tend to start talking more and listening less. This, he says, is the death knell to innovation. He reminds us that while seeing and listening are perceptions ... speaking is not.

Active vs. Passive Perception

Within the broader study of psychology is a field of study referred to as ecological psychology, or environmental psychology. As the terms suggest, it is the study of human behavior in the actual environment (as opposed to a laboratory). And within that domain, there have been studies by psychologists, such as James J. Gibson or Roger G. Barker back in the 1970s, which led to the distinction between "active" and "passive" perception. On its surface, that may seem somewhat academic or esoteric, but if you were designing a robot to explore the bottom of the ocean, would you design it to simply provide a window into the ocean floor, or would you want it to take some form of action when it sees certain objects?

It is somewhat ironic that in more recent times, probably the biggest beneficiaries of this field of study has been in the field of robotics or in the creation of video games. For the rest of us, however, it pertains to how we employ our own perceptions.

As Robert Sutton challenges his readers, if you're in the business of innovation, don't just listen. *Really* listen. Don't just observe. *Really* observe.

Find the Pain

Clarkston Consulting is a U.S.-based firm that has had a hand in the creative undertakings of companies such as Coca Cola, Pfizer Pharmaceuticals and Estee Lauder Designs. Tom Finnegan, its CEO and co-founder, says creativity and innovation are nothing but active perceptions looking for pain points. Some are huge. Some are almost insignificant.

In many cases, he says, breakthrough innovations are the result of "creative re-combinations that come from unexpected places." We're in the business of looking for problems. And when we find one, we follow the path of problem-idea-strategy-plan, in that order.

How did Netflix address the problem of the hassle of renting movies and the pain of rental late fees? They re-invented the movie rental business.

Bryan Cheung echoes the point. He is the CEO and co-founder of Liferay, Inc, and author of the book, *How Innovation Happens.*

Put your perception to work and listen and observe. Find your customers' real needs, not just what they ask for, he says.

The truly groundbreaking products are those that address real pain points for real people.

And in most cases, they themselves don't know what that is.

Conclusion

Creativity, we learned, is not just a result of seeing things often enough and long enough, but seeing things differently. The longer Orville and Wilbur Wright stared at birds flying, the more they wondered how they flew. But when they could envision a bicycle not just on the roads, but flying in the air, they could conceptualize flying machines. It took going to India to study spiritualism and hearing new forms of music and instruments, such as the sitar, for the Beatles to conceive *Sgt. Pepper's Lonely Hearts Club Band*.

Whereas our perception helps us formulate our beliefs and guides us in and out of dangerous harbors, it can also be an inhibitor to creativity.

The world as we have created it is a process of our thinking. It cannot be changed without changing our thinking.

Albert Einstein

Our ability to suspend our beliefs is a critical skill in creating something new that never before existed. From da Vinci, to Edison, to Tesla, to the Wright Brothers, up to Steve Jobs, Mark Cuban and Elon Musk, their creations defied the conventional beliefs of the time, and in some cases, their own.

It is our perceptions that get us to the door of creativity, we learned, but in order to open that door, we must leave them behind. Only then will the creative process do its work.

Chapter Ten
Perception and Critical Thinking

Instead of teaching students what to think, we should be teaching students how to think.

Albert Einstein

Introduction

"Critical thinking," as opposed to just thinking is the difference between having a destination versus just riding around. It is the difference between theory and fact. In a court of law, it is in most cases, the difference between a conviction and an acquittal.

Using the same principle that lawyers and detectives are held accountable to in legal proceedings, critical thinking is being able to back up your argument with logic and facts. The standard, "beyond a reasonable doubt" as it is applied in a criminal trial, is not necessarily the same standard used in the workplace, but it's pretty close. And not a bad standard to apply.

The art and science of critical thinking has been studied in academic circles for a long time. It is believed that Francis Bacon wrote the first book on critical thinking, *The Advancement of Learning*, in 1605. In it, he concluded that much of human thought was "irrational," and was determined to establish new habits of thought in the education process. He put forth the need for a higher standard of thinking, which led to the notion of not just thinking about a subject, but thinking critically about it:

What are the facts that support your argument?

What is the source of your information?

How did you come to that conclusion?'

In other words, how do you justify your thinking? At times, we find ourselves capable of evaluating this on our own, whereas in other circumstances, we are challenged by others. But in either case, our critical thinking mechanisms are turned on.

If this is going to be a compelling, and more importantly, a credible read for you, for example, we must back up our own propositions with the same level of thought, logic and documentation. We have to apply critical thinking to the subject of critical thinking.

So the question is, how do our perceptions alter, shape or influence our ability to think critically? To what extent does our thought process remain true to the facts? And to what extent do our perceptions color those facts, or even take the place of facts?

Was Nelson Mandela a terrorist, or a statesman? Or both? What do we think? And what do the facts say?

And on the flip side, to what extent do the facts alter our perceptions?

Is Islam a religion of peace or violence? What do we think?

Critical thinking is the ability to look beyond opinions, theories or intuition, and apply facts and logic to form conclusions … to go beyond opinions to get to educated opinions. Do our perceptions get in the way, or do they enhance our ability to think critically?

What are the facts that will help us get to the answers?

Red Fernan works as a Christian youth center director, and

when not playing video games and writing poetry, he devotes his time to analyzing ways to get his adolescent subjects to be a little more critical in their thinking, as opposed to just spontaneously spouting unfounded hearsay as fact. He wrote a very interesting treatise on the subject, titled, *The Effect of Perception to Human Thinking and Behavior.* He concluded his study and his article this way:

The information that any person acquires from his or her perceptions achieves one of two outcomes.... It could alter what and how he or she thinks about a certain subject, an effect known as a paradigm shift. Or, it could fortify the current attitude or mindset resulting in a status quo.

So, the first thing we learn about our perceptions when we apply critical thinking is, (a) we either become more enlightened, thus altering our previous viewpoint; or, (b) we hold more dearly to the viewpoint we previously held ... but now with facts to back it up.

David Meltzer is CEO of Sports 1 Marketing and a public speaker, and has authored multiple books on the topic. One of them is titled *Game Time Decision Making: High-Scoring Business Strategies from the Biggest Names in Sports.* In a recent talk he gave to business leaders, he described the relationship between our perceptions and critical thinking this way, "Our thought process is the cause, and our perceptions are the effect." In other words, how we perceive things is governed by how much or how little thought we put into them. He went on to cite that critical thinking is essential if we are to have any type of credibility. That especially holds true in business or in public life, and especially in these days and the increased prevalence of "fact checkers." Just ask anyone who's made a public declaration only to be publicly corrected before the day was out.

So, where does the discipline of critical thinking begin?

Nature or Nurture?
So, which is it?

Daniel Kahneman, the renowned psychologist and winner of the Nobel Prize in Economics, wrote the *New York Times'* best seller, *Thinking, Fast and Slow.* In it, he explains, there are two systems that drive the way we think. The first, he says, is fast, intuitive, and emotional. The second is slower, more deliberative, and more logical. That is where the critical thinking occurs.

It is our fast thinking that typically guides us through the routine issues of our day: what clothes to wear, where to go to lunch, what to do this weekend, etc. However, if we fail to cultivate the second, the more deliberate part of our thought process, we can find ourselves applying the same, intuitive, "gut reaction" to more significant issues, from buying a home to determining a corporate strategy. That, Kahneman says, is where we can get into trouble.

Maria Konnikova is a Russian-American psychologist and author of the best-seller, *Mastermind: How to Think like Sherlock Holmes.* She describes those same two modes of thinking using the character made famous by Sir Arthur Conan Doyle, and his famous sidekick, Dr. Watson. She provides examples of how Holmes is deliberate and analytical, and by contrast, examples of how Dr. Watson is just the opposite ... more spontaneous and reactionary in drawing conclusions.

She says where Dr. Watson only sees, Holmes, she says, "sees and observes."

Echoing the same principle as Kahneman, Konnikova says, "Our minds have two distinct modes of thought. The first of these modes operates quickly and automatically. It is our default mode. It is the one that we rely on as a matter of course. While it may be quick and effortless, it is also very error-prone. Our second mode of thought is slower and more deliberate. It has the potential to be far more accurate than our default mode, but it takes effort."

She describes the process of training that second, more fact-based part of our thinking as being no different than training any other part of our body. Exercising the brain to examine issues more methodically breeds brain power. Eventually, she says, that way of thinking becomes a habit.

So, which one is it? Critical thinking, according to our experts, is not an innate characteristic, but a trained discipline. No different than lifting weights or conducting cardio exercises for our physical bodies, it must be cultivated and trained, and eventually becomes habit forming. Since we're not born with it, the discipline of critical thinking has to be taught ... by our parents, by our community, and hopefully, in our schools. And never too early.

Training the Brain to Think Critically

As Mr. McClellan's eighth-grade students were settling in to their afternoon Modern History class, one of the students, fourteen-year-old Gregory Fields, proclaimed to all who were in earshot,

"Did you know that when they said that astronauts landed on the moon, it was really on a mountain that just looked like the moon? The whole thing was staged!!!" His teacher, who was also in earshot, was somewhat taken aback and curious by his student's declaration.

Mr. McClellan asked, "Gregory, where did you hear that?"

Pointing to his classmate, Gregory matter-of-factly replied, "Randy told me."

Then, looking at Randy, the teacher asked, "Randy, where did you hear this?"

With the same matter-of-fact tone, Randy said, "Well, it's all over the internet."

The absurdity of Randy's response was not lost on his teacher. It was a stark reminder to him that his eighth-grade class had not received any formal training on the topic of critical thinking at this point in their education. So, he viewed the situation as a teachable moment, and decided to capitalize on the opportunity.

The liberal arts teacher was reminded of a hypothesis he had formulated from his many years as a teacher and as a parent. He had long concluded that adolescents (and many adults) can be easily swayed by rumor, innuendo, half-truths and conspiracy theories with little or no in-depth investigation on their own.

He decided this would be a perfect opportunity to test the hypothesis further, with his class. He continued the discussion, and incorporated the remaining members of his class, who were already listening intently.

"What about you, Chip? Do you think the moon landing was a hoax, too?" Chip was both a classmate and close friend to Gregory and Randy. The teacher knew they were friends and had probably participated in the same hallway conversations.

"Well, I never thought anything about it until I heard these rumors. I don't know. It could be true," he responded with a shrug of his shoulders. (Chip was not known to be a deep thinker.)

"Anyone else? Does anybody else in the class have an opinion one way or the other, on the moon landing being a hoax?"

Sarah Bartlett, after scanning around the room and seeing no others respond, slowly raised her hand. She was Mr. McClellan's best student, and possibly the smartest person in the entire eighth grade. She said, "We've heard these kinds of theories before, but I was under the impression that they had all been de-bunked as just hoaxes."

Mr. McClellan devoted the entire fifty-minute class to the topic of theories, hoaxes, and unsubstantiated facts, framing the discourse around the central question, "How do we get to the truth?"

Having come to no clear conclusion, at the end of the class period, he decided to extend the exchange even further, by giving his class an impromptu overnight assignment.

"Tonight, your homework assignment," he told his class, "is to do a little research to determine if the moon landing was a hoax, or if our astronauts truly landed on the moon. I want a minimum of four reputable sources to substantiate your conclusions. I want you to be able to cite each of your sources with any commentary about their credibility, and be prepared to give a five-minute summary of your findings."

The following day, as his Modern History students arrived for the 2:10 class, Mr. McClellan pulled Gregory Fields aside to confirm he had completed the assignment (Gregory said he had) and to inform him he would be the first to be called on give his report.

Gregory didn't disappoint. He began his report by saying that he (and his friend, Randy) had been wrong in their earlier conclusions. He then went on to cite multiple sources that offered various conspiracy theories about the moon landing, but each had been refuted by other, more credible sources. "Each of these conspiracy theories appear to have been made by websites who tend to thrive on conspiracy theories, from the moon landing to the attacks on 9/11."

Though the topic of critical thinking had not been on the course agenda, or even a part of the Modern History curriculum, Mr. McClellan had just introduced his class to the concept of critical thinking. From this impromptu introduction, the teacher explained that he was giving the students a brief glimpse into what they should expect, both in their continued education, and in the world of work.

And in Higher Education?

As technology has dramatically increased the amount of data we are subjected to, both credible and incredible, education systems around the world are attempting to place a greater emphasis on the discipline of critical thinking. Those efforts can be found in the form of research projects, term papers, theses, and doctoral dissertations.

The assignments are designed to require students to apply critical thinking to make their case. What is your premise? What are the facts to back it up? What methodology did you use? To students, these assignments can seem like elaborate and painful, "make-work" exercises. But in reality, they are not only designed to increase subject matter expertise, but to also instill the practice of critical thinking ... especially in preparation to enter the workforce.

Colleges and universities around the world are placing a greater emphasis on critical thinking. And, thus far, as much increased focus as the subject has received, more is expected, both in terms of the effectiveness of their efforts, and the methods they employ.

In a recent study performed by Martha L. A. Stassen, Anne Herrington, and Laura Henderson, from the University of Massachusetts Amherst, the three concluded, "Critical thinking is an important learning outcome for higher education. Yet the definitions and the assessment instruments that are used on campuses continue to vary."

Feeling the heat from employers, the ultimate recipients of the students being trained, educational institutions and associations within the higher education community are continuously working to develop ways to improve. The principles of critical thinking have become a major focus in the higher education community.

Meanwhile, as academicians work to improve on the subject, the demand from employers is greater than ever.

In the Workplace

Michael Kallet is the author of *Think Smarter: Critical Thinking to Improve Problem-Solving and Decision-Making Skills.* He is also the CEO of Headscratchers, a firm he founded in 2004 to train individuals and organizations how to apply critical thinking in their business environments.

Kallet says in his forty-plus years in working with companies, from start-ups to Fortune 50 corporations, he has seen two ingredients that were present in those companies that were deemed successful. "The first," he said, "was persistence." They would always find a way, he said. "The second ingredient was quality thinking: real, hard, rollup-the-sleeves, not-taking-anything-for-granted critical thinking."

He talked of how effective leaders, even when they knew the answer, would ask questions and challenge their teams to propose solutions. They would then, he said, challenge team members to substantiate their opinions with facts with research.

Critical thinking, Kallet says, doesn't necessarily make you more intelligent. But it sure makes you smarter and more confident about your decisions.

Steve Siebold is the author of eight books, all centered on the theme of mental toughness, which also happens to be the title of one of his books. He is the CEO of Siebold Success Network. He, his books and his training, all describe the discipline of critical thinking as a core essential to any type of business or life success. He describes critical thinking as "the ability to remove all emotion from an issue; observe the facts objectively; and make a logical decision."

Critical thinking, he says, is as essential as the other core qualities of effective leadership, from emotional intelligence, to decision making, to conflict management. "Amateurs operate on whimsy and delusion," he says. "Pros operate on facts and objective reality."

So, why do employers place so much emphasis on critical thinking? Executive coach and leadership consultant Dave

Gambrill says the primary reason is real simple. Contrary to the popular notion that employers want to make all the decisions themselves, what they really want is to be able to trust their employees to make tough decisions. "Leaders don't want to micromanage their employees," he said, "but often they are forced to because the employees lack critical thinking skills."

Whether making decisions about which customer to call on, or which markets to pursue or abandon, the same discipline is required. Critical thinking is the difference between making decisions, and making *informed* decisions.

There is still too much of a tendency to apply that fast, mindless and spontaneous mode of thinking in the workplace, says Jen Lawrence, another leadership coach and co-author of the book, *Engage the Fox: A Business Fable About Thinking Critically and Motivating Your Team.* She asks a simple question, "How many times have you responded too quickly to a message or made a hasty business decision, only to find that you needed to correct yourself later because you didn't think it all the way through?"

The author cites how the seemingly increasing frequency of these types of incidents waste valuable time in the workplace. "Everyone is incredibly busy, and often we believe that we don't have the time to really think through an issue. However, using a structured thinking process actually saves time in the long run."

Conclusion

So, critical thinking is just that ... a thought process supported by critical examination. It is not something that we're born with. We have to cultivate it. In some cases, extensive research is required. In other instances, a quick check with Siri may suffice. Like a good news reporter ... what are the facts of my story, and what are the sources that substantiate those facts?

We all know a Cliff Claven, the postal-carrying barfly character from the popular television series, *Cheers.* The one who knows something about everything, and has an opinion on everything. What we don't know, however, is how much of his opinions and insights were substantiated by facts or documentation, and how much were the ponderings of a smart, if slightly misguided individual.

Everyday businesses are at risk of making critical decisions based on the Cliff Clavens in their office. Every day, we run the risk of the loudest opinion ruling the day, which is not always the smartest. We are all at risk of declaring our perceptions not to be opinions or "points of view," but to be fact. Or, to allow others to sway us because theirs is the loudest opinion in the room.

From our previous teachings and work with organizations, we have found numerous ways to encourage more critical thinking within the workforce. One of those, for example, was to have employees research and present a relevant topic of their choice at a weekly meeting. Topics included everything from ways to improve how the organization performs certain tasks to how to get employees more engaged in their work. Similarly, have employees develop expertise and become a subject matter expert to explain an area that interests them that no one else really knows well.

A time-tested way for employees to expand their expertise is to have them research a topic and teach it. That same principle applies to encouraging critical thinking.

It is our critical thinking that keeps us on safe ground. It is our critical thinking that allows us to stay the course. It is our critical thinking that takes us closer to that society that Sir Francis Bacon envisioned back in 1605.

Chapter Eleven
Perception and Curiosity

Our perceptions suggest that we know something; our curiosity proves that we don't.

Descartes

Introduction

In examining how perception impacts our skills, abilities and attributes in the workplace, perhaps none was as prevalent in our examination as was the intersection between perception and curiosity. If perception is the assumption of knowledge, then curiosity is its validation, or invalidation. As many describe them, they are the sister underpinnings of knowledge.

So, how do the two work together?

In 2011, behavioral scientists Freda-Marie Hartung and Britta Renner conducted a study to examine how our curiosity affects our perceptions about others. In the study, they asked 182 individuals that had undergone a series of personality tests to meet for ten minutes with individuals they had never met before; and then, after the interview, to evaluate their perceptions of the other individual.

The results showed that those individuals who were judged to be "highly perceptive" by virtue of previous assessments, were also deemed to be "highly curious." They demonstrated much more knowledge and understanding of their fellow subject, as evidenced by more accurate recall and insights about their partner's traits and personality.

This was one of many examples we found about how the two characteristics influence one another. In her examination of the subject, as chronicled in her previous publication, *Cracking the Curiosity Code,* author Dr. Diane Hamilton noted that age is another factor in the connection between curiosity and perception.

"As we grow older," Hamilton states, "we become more comfortable with our surroundings and our experiences, which, in turn, shape our perceptions." This phenomenon can therefore lessen our curiosity as we begin to rely more on our past experiences and less on a further pursuit of knowledge. "When faced with an unfamiliar situation or a problem, our minds perceive it as a gap, a place of confusion or conflict. To resolve this discrepancy, our mind naturally tends to fill in the blanks with information from our past experiences."

Her conclusions corroborate numerous other studies that have cited the influence of age as a factor in the curiosity/ perception phenomenon. The consensus seems to be that the older and the more entrenched we become with our perceptions, the less curious we become. The inverse, those studies indicate, can also be true.

Hamilton cites fear and apprehension as yet another factor that can influence our curiosity. From her previous writings on the subject, Dr. Hamilton tells us how fear can impact our curiosity, vis-à-vis our perceptions. In the physical sense, we may be reluctant to venture into unfamiliar territory or new unknown situations because of fear. In the social sense, if we are fearful or apprehensive about how we may be perceived by others, we might be reluctant to ask questions, thus inhibiting our curiosity, especially in circumstances where we may be uncertain of our surroundings.

There are numerous examples such as these that illustrate how our curiosity can affect our perceptions, and vice-versa. So, what does all that mean in the context of our day-to-day behavior, or in the workplace?

Let's start with the premise that we each approach situations with a boatload of perceptions, biases and opinions, from our cultural upbringing, to our last job, or our education, among other things.

How many times have you heard, "Well, that's not the way we did it at_____"?

As we concluded in the chapter on Collaboration, we noted that if we're not careful, our perceptions can guide us into some major obstacles to working well with others. Well, what we learned here is that curiosity can be the key to navigating around those obstacles.

That's another thing we've learned about curiosity … it can rescue us when our perceptions take us into blind alleyways.

If the question is, "How do I get diverse teams to work more effectively together?" Or, "How do I become more productive?" Or, "How do I get a promotion?" chances are, the answer, in one way or another, is going to include curiosity.

Working with people whose motivations you don't quite understand? Curiosity will help you understand them better.

The boss has given you a ridiculous assignment? Curiosity is the key to finding the answer.

Feeling a little bored with your job? Curiosity will reignite your interests, or take you where your interests reside.

With all this build-up about curiosity, you might think we're suggesting that curiosity is like a "one size fits all" solution to all our problems. Well, the scientific research on the subject tells us it is far more complex than that. But for the purposes of this discussion, let's go with that. After all, our objective is not to educate you on all the scientific intricacies of curiosity, but simply to understand the relationship between perception and curiosity. And we emphasize the word, "simply."

But to achieve that objective, a little bit of those scientific intricacies will be needed. So, let's begin with a little brain science, and then break it down from there.

We begin with an introduction to Dr. Todd Maddox, the CEO and founder of Cognitive Design and Statistical Consulting. He has published more than 200 scientific articles, resulting in more than 10,000 academic citations, all looking at various aspects of how our brains behave as they are constantly being bombarded with stimuli.

The first point he makes is that our brains are continually taking in sensory input via our collective auditory, visual, tactile, and olfactory senses. However, he says, only a certain amount of that input reaches the conscious brain. Much of it falls outside the realm of our conscious thought and never registers, generally because our focus is elsewhere. The data is still being received, and still being stored in our brains, but not at a conscious level. That's one piece of the equation.

The second, he says, is that the sensory input that does make it into our conscious brains is a relatively small subset of the total. That small subset is the input that becomes our "perceptions." And, that is the subset that triggers, or fails to trigger, our curiosity.

The third point he makes is that even those subconscious elements that are absorbed into the brain, but fail to register, can also subliminally trigger perceptions.

That is like the roadside sign that you pass every day on your way to work. It is captured by your visual senses, but because your mind is elsewhere, it fails to register with your conscious brain. However, your brain has sub-consciously captured and cataloged that image. So, it is not uncommon when, later in the day or that night in your dreams, you think about the law firm of "Johnson and Johnson," and have no idea why!

That is our first lesson about perception and curiosity. The second is about why some of our perceptions make us curious, and others do not.

Dr. George Loewenstein is the director of the Center for Behavioral Decision Research at Carnegie Mellon University, and a leader in the fields of behavioral economics and neuroeconomics. Now if that doesn't impress you, we'll also tell you he is the great-grandson of Sigmund Freud. After all, his full name is George Freud Lowenstein. Whether it's coincidence or genetics, he also happens to be one of the great minds in the study of curiosity.

He defined curiosity as, "a cognitive induced deprivation that arises from the perception of a gap in knowledge and understanding."

So, what does that mean? Lowenstein formulated the "information gap" theory that says simply that curiosity is just like other bodily functions, such as hunger. When you're hungry, you eat. And when you eat enough, you become satiated and are no longer hungry. Likewise, when you're curious, you seek! And when you find what you were seeking, you're no longer curious!

So, if we apply the information gap theory, how does that connect to perception?

With perception being what we see, hear, read, etc., if for whatever reason we are dissatisfied, or feel a sense of deprivation about any aspect of what we've seen, heard or read, etc., then it is our curiosity that motivates us to resolve that dissatisfaction. If, for example, I read in the news about Bastille Day in France, and can't remember the origins or the purpose of Bastille Day, it is my curiosity that prompts me to find out. In other words, if our perception is where we are, and we're not satisfied, then our curiosity is the vehicle that leads us to what we seek.

So, with that as a very simplified foundation, let's see what we're told about why we are curious about some things and uncurious about others; and, how some people are *very* curious, and some not curious at all.

Curiosity doesn't magically take us out of the dark, but it does provide us a flashlight.

There appears to be a strange paradox in the workplace when it comes to the topic of curiosity. Its benefits have been well documented, i.e., we're more creative, more productive, work more effectively in teams, etc. when we are curious. Francesca Gino is a professor at Harvard Business School and founder and CEO of Feel Logic. Her work on the subject of curiosity was chronicled in her book, *Rebel Talent.* In a recent interview, she told us that curiosity is even more important to the success of an enterprise than previously thought.

Gino says when curiosity is triggered, "we think more deeply and rationally about decisions and come up with more-creative solutions. In addition, curiosity allows leaders to gain more respect from their followers and inspires employees to develop more trusting and more collaborative relationships with their colleagues."

She says organizations that encourage curiosity see improvements not only in creativity, but in problem solving, empathy and teambuilding. With curiosity, she says, we are less likely to fall prey to obstacles such as confirmation bias (looking for information that only supports what we already believe) and stereotyping people (you know, those broad judgments, such as thinking women or minorities don't make good leaders).

The benefits, she says, are endless. So, with that, you would think that every organization would be pushing for more curiosity in their work environment. Yet, many managers tend to discourage their workers from practicing curiosity. They tend to discourage anything that is outside the norm of existing processes and controls. Thinking outside the box, they fear, can lead to conflicts, time-consuming debates and pushing against the status quo.

So, what gives?

Well, according to Gino, many of those same leaders say they value curiosity in their workforce, but her research findings suggest just the opposite. She says what leaders really value is order and control, which flies in the face of curiosity. And this is where perception kicks in.

Because of the fear of those perceived conflicts and debates, which lead to disorganization or loss of control, there is a tendency to stifle curiosity. In a survey she conducted of more than 3,000 employees from a wide range of firms and industries, she said only about 24% reported feeling encouraged to be curious in their jobs, while about 70% said they are discouraged from asking questions. Based on the research she's conducted, many managers seem to have a "just do your job" attitude, as opposed to anything that might disrupt the status quo.

For the more conventional leader, she says, the very notion of fostering an environment of curiosity is alien to their traditional leadership norms. Many managers and top executives have risen through the ranks by providing "fixes and solutions," and not by asking questions. And once they've attained a position of leadership, they may feel the need to manage the same way by projecting confident expertise. To acknowledge uncertainty by asking questions carries the risk that the leader could be perceived as lacking knowledge.

(We'll see how long this attitude can last, as Millennials and Gen Xers are fast replacing Baby Boomers in the workforce. And, they ask more questions than your five-year-old whose favorite word is "why.")

So, what's the answer? In addition to the emergence of a more curious–and, some will say, more creative–workforce, many experts tell us the magic formula comes down to two words: humility and confidence.

For one, Tenelle Porter says, managers need to demonstrate "higher levels of intellectual humility." Porter, a postdoctoral scholar at the University of California, Davis, describes intellectual humility as the "willingness to consider views other than your own."

Secondly, as authors Clayton Christensen, Hal Gregersen and Jeff Dyer wrote in their book *The Innovator's DNA,* the more-effective leaders they studied seemed to demonstrate a rare blend of humility and confidence. They were humble enough to acknowledge that they didn't have all the answers, and confident enough to be able to admit that in front of everyone else.

That combination of humility and confidence became a recurring theme in our research.

Paul Polman, CEO of Unilever said, "The issues we face today are so big and so challenging that we cannot do it alone, so there is a certain humility and a recognition that we need to invite other people in and be comfortable enough in saying we don't have all the answers."

Once again, that is where perception comes in. Your colleagues are watching. No matter your position in the organization, if you are perceived as displaying that combination of humility and confidence, chances are you are fostering an environment that invites curiosity and leadership. So, how do those leaders tend to exhibit that combination of humility and confidence? What is it they do differently?

For that, we looked to Kevin Cashman, who is a senior partner and CEO for Executive Development at Korn Ferry, the world's leading executive search firm, and perhaps one of the foremost expert organizations when it comes to assessing talent. Cashman has also authored multiple books on the subject, including, *Leadership from the Inside Out* and *The Pause Principle*. He told us that those managers who foster curiosity do two simple things: they are masters at the art of "asking questions and listening."

It's amazing, he told us, the power and credibility that those two simple behaviors impart. "Questions," he said, "are the expressive, probing language; and listening is the receptive, facilitating language. Combined, these two behaviors are the key to leadership development."

To further the point, he described a survey his firm conducted of more than one thousand CEOs. Of the most vital traits required in today's workforce, a majority of respondents cited traits such as curiosity and open mindedness as being vital, especially as the work environment becomes increasingly technical, more competitive and more complex.

One of those respondents, McCormick & Company CEO Alan D. Wilson, said, "the business leaders who are always expanding their perspective and encourage curiosity in their workforce are the ones who are going to be successful. Examine the attributes of a successful leader," he says, "and you'll find curiosity at or near the top."

Francesca Gino perhaps said it best. The famed behavioral scientist and author of *Sidetracked: Why Our Decisions Get Derailed, and How We Can Stick to the Plan*, said, "It turns out that curiosity seems to be more important in today's organization than we once thought. That means all organizations, from Zimbabwe to Hollywood."

Speaking of Hollywood, the famed movie producer Brian Grazer is an ardent champion of the art of asking questions and listening. He wrote in his book, *A Curious Mind,* "If you're the boss, and you manage by asking questions, you're laying the foundation for the culture of your company or your group." Tagging on to the traditional management phrase, "management by objectives" or its many variations, Grazer offers another variation: management by curiosity. He states that leading by curiosity can help generate more ideas from all areas of an organization, while also helping to raise employee engagement levels.

Warren Berger has written extensively on the subjects of creativity and innovation, and authored the book, *A More Beautiful Question.* In it, he reminds us that the notion of curiosity, while perhaps more critical than ever, is not entirely new. He reflects that Walt Disney declared that his company managed to keep innovating "because we remain curious, and curiosity is what keeps leading us down new paths."

While conducting research for his book, Berger uncovered numerous examples where leaders and CEOs, including Netflix's Reed Hastings, Square's Jack Dorsey, and the team behind Airbnb, all relied on a strong curiosity as the foundation for creating new companies and reinventing entire industries.

Berger tells the story of how Dorsey was curious as to why an artist friend lost a big sale to a potential customer simply because the artist couldn't accept a credit card. Dorsey disliked the fact that only established businesses, and not smaller entrepreneurs, were able to conduct credit card transactions. It was that curiosity which resulted in the creation of Square, a more accessible credit card reader. He cited that an endless desire to explore "new paths" becomes even more important in today's fast-changing, innovation-driven marketplace.

Dave Ulrich is known as the Father of Modern HR and author of thirty books and more than 200 articles about leadership. In a recent interview, he echoed the same sentiments as one of the previously mentioned authors, John Maxwell, whom we quoted in the chapter on Failure, advocating the traits of curiosity, experimentation, and the concept of "failing forward." He described the importance of curiosity not about an event, but of the process leading up to the event. "What did we learn along the way?... about how we got here?"

Finally, Ron Shaich, CEO of Panera Bread, reinforces the point that curiosity is not just for start-up companies or wiz-bang entrepreneurs. He says that, given the dynamics of today's marketplace, curiosity is essential to the survival of anyone in any business, and our perceptions should guide us to be more curious, not less. "Every day," he says, "a new competitor arrives on the horizon, and every day it takes new ideas to retain whatever competitive edge you may have; even if you bring them from other cultures, other industries, or even outside the business world."

> *All that we take in, what we see, what we hear, what we smell, taste and touch, makes us either more or less curious.*
>
> *Author Unknown*

Conclusion

In examining the many studies on the subject, we learned that curiosity is not the linchpin of our perceptions, but the linchpin of our *informed* perceptions. We further learned that the symbiotic relationship between curiosity and perception goes far beyond knowledge. The two form a partnership to affect emotions such as happiness, joy, and a sense of well-being.

Again, quoting Dr. Diane Hamilton in her interview with Francesca Gino, the two conclude, "One of the key ingredients of a happy life and feeling content is staying curious. Curiosity makes people search for answers and meaning, which later on lead them to self-perceptions of happiness, growth, and further exploration."

Silvia Garcia, CEO of Happiest Places to Work, echoes the sentiment. In her interview, she said, "If staying curious helps our brains release dopamine because we discover new things, then it is definitely a good source of happiness."

Want to be smarter? Want to see things clearer? Want to feel the dopamine effects of feeling more knowledgeable and feeling better about yourself and the world around you?

Then, remain curious!

Chapter Twelve
Perception and Decision Making

If you obsess over whether you are making the right decision, you are basically assuming that the universe will reward you for one thing and punish you for another.

Deepak Chopra

Introduction

Decision making, according to the behaviorists, should be an outgrowth of critical thinking. (As we know, not all decisions are well thought out.) Good decisions should be the result of intelligent analysis of the problem and its options. On the other hand, many will argue that you don't need to know all the facts to make an intelligent decision. In fact, they argue that too many facts can get in the way.

We know examples of colossal failures that were the result of a wide range of possible alternatives, detailed analysis, and intelligent, informed decisions. From the Edsel to Enron, industry is full of them. Then, we know of examples where brilliant decisions resulted not from in-depth analysis, but from the "gut," or intuition. Velcro, sticky notes and the microwave were all results of accidents, or on a hunch.

So which is it? Or does it depend on other variables? Author C.S. Lewis said, "What you see and hear depends a great deal on where you are standing. It also depends on what sort of person you are." Assuming that is true, our decision making is certainly influenced accordingly. In other words, "Where you stand depends on where you sit."

Wherever you are sitting, your perceptions are playing a large role in your decision making.

Perception's Impact on Our Decision Making

Let's start with the basics. The classic decision-making process is described as having the following basic steps:

1. Define the problem or issue.

2. Define the goal or resolution.

3. Generate alternative solutions that could achieve that goal.

4. Analyze and decide which alternative best achieves the goal.

5. Implement the selected alternative.

Sounds simple, right? Invariably, decisions are reduced down to two alternatives, "A" or "B," chocolate or vanilla, the red one or the blue one. But other situations are not so simple and require looking beyond options A or B to find a third option.

Critical thinking, researchers tell us, is essential to making informed decisions. It can also tell us the plusses and minuses of different alternative options. But critical thinking does not make the decision for us. That is where intuition steps in.

So, how does our perception aid or inhibit our decision-making ability? This is what we found out.

Pre-Decision Making

Dr. Robert Cialdini is the Regents' Professor Emeritus of Psychology and Marketing at Arizona State University and author of the book, *Pre-Suasion*. His findings suggest that our perceptions play a large role in our decision making even before the event. In essence, there are factors that are at work, almost imperceptibly, pre-conditioning us as we make choices. In some cases, he says, it can be sounds and in other instances, large numbers, or any variety of sensory perceptions.

For example, he cites studies that show individuals are more inclined to spend more for a dinner when the restaurant was named Studio 97 as opposed to Studio 17. In other instances, people were shown to be willing to pay more for a box of Belgian chocolates after being asked to write down a pair of high numbers versus low numbers. Even in the area of research, the results of an experiment were predicted to be better when the experiment was labeled experiment 27 vs. experiment 9.

In terms of sounds, experimenters found that customers in a wine shop were more likely to purchase a German vintage if, before deciding, they heard a German song playing on the shop's sound system. The same was found to be true when considering a French wine if the song were French.

In order to persuade others, Cialdini concludes, it is necessary to *pre-suade,* as he describes it. Set the stage, he says. But how? He says the answer lies in a profound but often overlooked tenet: "What we present first, shapes the way people experience what we present to them next."

From the scientific perspective, he explains that our perceptions and our activities are not a result of isolated neural events, but a result of a pattern of mental associations. What we experience before making decisions carries over to the decision-making process itself.

Throughout the entire process–before, during, and after we make decisions–our perceptions are at work. Whether it is which wine to buy, which job to take, or which neighborhood to live in, our perceptions, both consciously and subconsciously, are influencing us in one direction or another.

Perception's Role

> *The observing eye sees what is.*
> *The perceiving eye is our interpretation.*
>
> **Musashi, Samurai Swordsman**

As author C.S. Lewis reminds us, our perceptions and, hence, our decision making, is heavily influenced by "where we stand" and our general outlook on life. The poets and philosophers through the ages have pointed out how our mindset, be it positive and optimistic, or dark and brooding, sets the tone for the way we perceive and the way we make decisions. Our outlook on life is shaped by how we interpret what we see and hear.

Many believe our decision making can be further influenced by what is referred to as the Laws of Attraction, an interesting, if not highly debated phenomenon. Proponents of the concept proclaim that if we channel and "re-train" our minds to cherry-pick and choose those perceptions that are favorable, we improve our ability to experience a favorable outcome, whereas others tend to pooh-pooh the subject. Dr. Neil Farber, a psychologist and adjunct professor of psychology at Arizona State University, in his 2016 article in *Psychology Today,* "The Truth About the Law of Attraction," says, "to invoke this concept, one needs to live in a continuous unreal future as you anticipate that and visualize only a successful outcome."

Proponents in the concept, however, teach us that if we are unable to visualize a positive outcome, due to negative thoughts or anxieties, our perceptions will lead us towards negative outcomes.

Either way, what we see and hear, and how we attempt to guide our perceptions of what we see and hear, are the basis of our decision making.

Let's begin with the most active of our perceptions: what we see.

As for visual perception, a group of psychologists from Duke University used the online game, Airport Scanner, to see if our visual perceptions are influenced by the frequency in which we see an object.

In the online game, players are presented a series of X-ray images of traveler's suitcases as they would appear to an airport security screener, and tasked with searching for illegal items in the simulated images. The contraband items in each piece of luggage could range from a variety of weapons, explosives, and other forms of illegal items a security screener would look for. Players view one bag at a time and use finger taps to identify the number of illegal items they find in each piece of luggage.

Various weapons, pieces of dynamite, hand grenades appear frequently and are typically identified by the players as contraband.

Items that do not appear frequently, such as a switchblade knife, screwdriver or a hammer, however, are more frequently missed by the participants and allowed to slip through.

Numerically, the researchers found a direct correlation between the subjects' ability to detect contraband items and the frequency in which they were shown. The players, the researchers concluded, are conditioned by the frequency to look for certain items, while overlooking the items that were less frequently shown.

So, what does that mean for the rest of us? It means that we are typically pretty competent at seeing what we're accustomed to look for; but we tend to be far less competent at detecting the unexpected. When it comes to our decision-making abilities, we can get lulled into considering and analyzing the more obvious choices, while overlooking those that are less obvious.

The lesson for us is to take a decision-making approach which is more diligent and more creative. The mantra being that the more options that are considered in making a decision, the better the outcome. Instead of considering either option A or option B, or even options A, B or C when considering decisions, chances are we're not looking deeply enough.

Maybe, if we are more diligent and more creative, there could be options D, E, F, or G.

OK, Maybe Not Always ... Perception Overload

Dr. Barry Schwartz cautions that there are times when more alternatives in the decision-making process are not always better. In his book, *The Paradox of Choice,* he explains how, in some cases, too much of a good thing can be detrimental to our psychological and emotional well-being. The professor of social theory and social action in the psychology department at Swarthmore College makes the counterintuitive case that eliminating choices in some situations can greatly reduce the stress, anxiety, and busyness of our lives.

For example, how many choices of ice cream will you offer your five-year-old child: the entire menu of flavors, or simply chocolate or vanilla?

Schwartz describes how the over-abundance of choices can lead to sensory overload, thus paralyzing the decision-making process. In those cases, he says, limit choices to a manageable number, have the discipline to focus on the important ones and ignore the rest. Ultimately, you and the subject will be happier, and derive greater satisfaction from the process and the choices you make.

One such example was made evident to a group of corporate executives as they tried to woo new customers. During the early break-up of the Soviet Union into separate countries during the 1980s, several U.S. multi-national companies who were in pursuit of this new potential market conducted tours and visits for government officials from several former Soviet-bloc countries. Their aim was to get the first-time visitors to realize the virtues of an American democracy and the wealth that could be achieved. They wanted the officials to see, firsthand, the abundance of the U.S. and the potential for these newly created countries.

On one such visit, a former Soviet executive was visiting a large supermarket where he saw an abundant selection of meats, fruits, vegetables and other items. The visitor was virtually overwhelmed at the site of the grocery shelves stocked full on every aisle.

Seeing the perplexed look on the visitor's face, his host asked him what was causing his concerned reaction. The visitor said, "Here, you have the freedom of choice. In our country, we have the freedom *from* choice. Up to now, our government decided where we lived, where we worked, and what to purchase. We were free of those decisions. I'm beginning to realize the challenges our people would have in this type of system."

And, What We Touch

Another study, by psychologists Joshua Ackerman, Christopher Nocera and John A. Bargh, found that the tactile touch of our hands also plays a large role in our decision-making. The three collaborators, from the Massachusetts Institute of Technology, Harvard University and Yale University, co-authored a study published in the *National Library of Medicine* in 2010, saying that the sensation of touch is one of the most underappreciated facets of our senses despite the fact that tactile sensations are critical to both our intrapersonal and interpersonal lives.

In their publication, titled "Incidental Haptic Sensations Influence Social Judgments and Decisions," they found a direct correlation between our haptic perceptions of touch and our decision making. For instance, shoppers are more inclined to buy items they can physically touch. The same, they found, is true about visual and taste perceptions. For example, subjects declared water appeared to taste better from a firm bottle than from a flimsy bottle. Further, they found that we tend to make judgments and decisions about the packaging of a product, which can even override our decisions about the quality of the product itself.

In all, they found that the weight of an object, the texture of an object, and the hardness of an object can each subconsciously influence our judgments and decisions about unrelated events, situations, and objects.

In conclusion, the psychologists tell us, the studies repeatedly showed that our sensory perception of touch exerts a broad influence over our decision making in ways of which we are probably often unaware.

Conclusion

As it turns out, all of our senses that shape our perceptions influence our decisions, both for better or worse. They either aid or inhibit. First off, in the simplest of terms, the more we know about a subject (or think we know), the less we are inclined to apply a rigorous process in analyzing and making decisions about the subject.

If I know (or think I know) a Toyota is a more reliable automobile than a Ford, I'm not inclined to do a deep dive into my analysis to relearn what I already know (or think I know). Conversely, if my mind is a blank slate on the issue, and have little or no preconceived notion about the subject, I may apply a little more rigor to the decision-making process.

As the famed psychologist R.D. Laing reminded us in his best-seller, *Knots,* "If I don't know, but don't know that I don't know, I think I know." (Yeah, we had to read it twice also). Our perception about what we know and what we think we know goes a long way in influencing how much more we want to find out and analyze, before we decide.

Studies have shown that, consciously or unconsciously, we tend to inject our own biases into both what we perceive and hence, the quality of the decision-making process. They cite several examples, such as selectively seeking information to justify certain decisions (confirmation bias). Or when we base decisions on limited, but readily available information (availability bias).

Or when we stand by a decision when it's been proven to be wrong (escalation bias) … you know, like when you're still convinced the suspect is guilty, even after the evidence has been disproven. Or, when you continue to defend your vote after your political candidate turns out to be a disaster.

The line where our perceptions end and where facts begin is a fine one, and many times indistinct. Getting the right information is the first challenge in making intelligent, informed decisions. Keeping that information separate from our perceptions and biases is the second.

The third … is putting all the facts, figures and creative options next to your gut instinct, and see where you come down. More times than not, when you do that, odds are pretty good that you'll know.

Chapter Thirteen
Perception and Engagement

When people are financially invested, they want a return.
When people are emotionally invested, they want to contribute.

Simon Sinek

Introduction

How committed are you to your job? Your company? Your employer? Do you actively take ideas to your boss to improve the way the business operates?

These are the types of questions human resource professionals and the corporate world put under the category of employee engagement, which has become a big and very expensive issue. Studies have shown, for example, that the vast majority of employees are either completely disengaged from their work, or only moderately engaged. That means that the remaining minority, who are considered actively engaged, are the ones keeping their company afloat. Not just in terms of generating the revenue, but solving the day-to-day problems, developing new products, coming up with new, innovative ideas; that is not a sustainable business model. It is for these reasons that business owners and human resource professionals are looking for ways to turn those numbers around.

So our question was, "How do our perceptions play in this dynamic?" What is it that we see, hear and feel that makes us more or less engaged in our work ... in our company? The answer, we found out, is a lot! And surprisingly enough, it has little to do with the size of our paycheck each week.

To examine this, let's begin with the brain.

David Lee, founder and principal at the human resource firm, HumanNature@Work, writes that, dating back to when cavemen were fighting for survival, the human brain has been hardwired to sense and remember negative things more than positive ones. It makes more of an impact on our brain when we see a snake than when we hear a bird singing. Positives are nice, but what can hurt us makes a stronger impression.

Fast-forward to today's workplace. We appreciate the positive experiences that we enjoy in the workplace, but we never forget the negative ones. I might not remember the $500 bonus I received last year, but I'll remember when my boss failed to mention my name when our project team was being recognized ten years ago.

When we are engaged, in our work and in our company, it's because we're being challenged; we're being recognized; we are made to feel that we matter; we are appreciated; and we have opportunities to advance and feel we're being well compensated.

We become disengaged usually for the exact opposite reasons … when we're not appreciated, when we're not challenged; when we're not recognized; when we don't think we matter. We become disengaged at work for many of the same reasons we become disengaged in our relationships. It's the same human condition. Only in the workplace, there's a paycheck involved. So, it's easy to pin our lack of engagement on that.

Even when it is about the paycheck, it tends not to be about how much we make, but how equitable it is. Am I being paid fairly? Is my paycheck in line with what others make that perform the same job as me? And is there opportunity for advancement?

So, how do we recognize those indicators that keep us engaged or disengaged? We get the paycheck thing. That's a tangible measure. But in the larger scheme of things, compensation seems to be less of a factor than you might think. What about all the other, more subtle things that we see and hear that cause us to be excited and committed to our work and our company, as opposed to having our eyes glued to job sites?

That is the focus of this chapter.

Appreciation is a wonderful thing. It makes what is excellent in others belong to us as well.

Voltaire

To begin, let's go back a few years to the early years when the technology boom was first beginning to disrupt old businesses and create new ones. In 1996, when the automation revolution was in its infancy and beginning to create new technology-based business models, the bloodbaths began.

We were learning how to use technology to do things that humans once did. Workers were being replaced by machines. In an effort to remain viable, competitive and productive in the new information economy, companies began using terms like "corporate reengineering" to engineer massive layoffs. Terms like downsizing or right-sizing came into vogue, and usually with little or no regard for the turmoil that was left in their wake.

Companies that were once bastions of strength, stability and lifetime employment, were reduced, both in size and in reputation, to mere shells of their former selves. Companies that were once considered a source of "good jobs" were no longer.

But then, there were other companies that managed to maintain their sense of stability and their reputations as reliable places to work. What were they doing differently? The Bain Consulting Company wanted to know.

Frederick Reichheld and a team of his fellow Bain consultants first calculated the losses of these re-engineering efforts. The numbers showed that companies were losing customers *(over half in less than five years)*, employees *(more than half every four years)*, and investors *(roughly half every year)*. The lost dollars that accompanied those losses were staggering.

After calculating the costs of the losses, they wanted to understand why they were occurring, and what could be done to reverse such an alarming trend. They began by examining those companies that were not experiencing those losses–companies such as Toyota, Lexus, State Farm, USAA, Chick-Fil-A and John Deere–to understand what they were doing that seemed to be making a difference.

What they found was captured in a book they called *The Loyalty Effect,* and it came down to one word... *engagement.*

The companies, such as Toyota, Lexus and State Farm, were all using different practices, but they were practices that were geared toward the same objectives ... ensure that their customers, their employees, and their investors felt actively involved in the success of the company and its employees. In other words, engaged.

The practices the authors uncovered certainly included compensation. But, they went far beyond compensation to include basic, elementary items, such as training, career development, recognition and retention practices.

They also discovered that those massive re-engineering efforts that companies had engaged in had done little to achieve any tangible gains in corporate performance. The financial gains they had achieved by reducing their workforce were offset by all the same factors that Kevin Sheridan outlined in his book, *Building a Magnetic Culture*. They found that the massive disruptions corporations hoped would improve their efficiency through their re-engineering efforts and layoffs actually had the exact opposite impact on morale, attrition and productivity. Further, those companies no longer had the reputation of being "a desirable place to work." They began to experience recruiting and retention problems. Even the employees they wanted to keep began to express second thoughts about their company.

The perceptions of employees and industry onlookers alike were working overtime, capturing the uncertainty of it all. Remember, the hard wiring of the brain ... we enjoy the nice things we experience, but we never forget those negative perceptions.

Instead of those companies being the pantheons of performance and stability they once were, they were cultivating reputations of companies to stay away from, due to the perceived uncertainty and chaos.

In contrast, the authors found companies such as USAA were achieving far greater yields by, instead of laying off their workforce, actually investing in their workforce. Employee training, career development and recognition programs were cited as the major factor that caused the company to increase its productivity more than one hundred times, with only a fivefold increase in its workforce. Reichheld summarized his study of USAA by stating, "The Company invests in employment and compensation policies that make their employees *want* to stay and produce."

Some twenty years after the initial publication of *The Loyalty Effect,* technologies have improved, and business practices have evolved and changed. Yet, multiple studies continue to show top performing companies separate themselves from the also-rans, not by throwing money at their employees, but by engaging them.

I guess we *do* like being treated like we matter.

But, what about our workforce as it has shifted from Baby Boomers to Millennials and Gen-Xers? That is a problem of a different type. Being treated like we matter seems to be more important than ever.

Millennials, the author says, love even more feedback and recognition than their Boomer predecessors ever received, or expected. Sheridan calculated that millennials look for compliments regarding their work as many as 12-14 times per day. In stark contrast, Baby Boomers, who climbed the corporate ranks in a very different time and culture, neither sought out that level of feedback, nor expected it. And, as managers, they don't feel compelled to provide that to their millennial employees.

Suck it up, Sheridan says. That's the world of productivity and engagement in the millennial world. If you cannot provide feedback to your employees 14 times per day, you should at least target 6 to 8 times per day. It is not about being nice, he says. It is essential in retaining talent and increasing productivity. He says, employees today look for basically three things:

1. Recognition
2. Career Development, and
3. Their relationship with their supervisor.

In addition to the recognition, employees cite career development, as they are eager to learn, grow, and expand their horizons, and they look for companies that provide a robust career development program.

As far as their relationship with their boss, think about it this way: how many of us are actively engaged in our company's performance, when we don't like the person we work for? Again, studies show this is not about the issue of likability. It is about human nature. How enjoyable is it to go to work, knowing your boss is unengaging, uninterested in you and your career, and difficult to get along with? And what if your boss were the opposite of those things?

Another proponent of employee engagement who sees the direct correlation between perception and employee engagement is Dr. Bob Nelson. He is a consultant on the subject to literally hundreds of companies, and has authored some twenty-nine books on the topic, including *1001 Ways to Motivate Employees* and *The Management Bible.*

In a recent interview on Dr. Diane Hamilton's show, Nelson stated that the key to engagement is recognition. This is a practice that many Baby Boomer managers, who were not trained to provide that level of constant feedback, have difficulty with. "Search for moments of positive achievements," Nelson says, "even small achievements, and recognize them immediately. Tomorrow or next week," he continues, "is too late. You will have lost the moment. Delayed recognition could even have a negative impact."

The author spoke of how he embraced the African proverb "Embutu" (*or Ubuntu*), roughly meaning, "I am because we are."

The 2008 world champion Boston Celtics embraced the

same philosophy, and even have the term engraved on their championship rings.

Earlier in this chapter, we mentioned the Gallup Organization and their numerous studies on the subject of engagement. Two of their consultants, Marcus Buckingham and Curt Coffman, conducted an extensive study to find the best management practices that tend to attract and retain talent and achieve high levels of productivity. They ask questions such as, "Should a good manager be able to identify good talent? Or should a good manager be able to groom talent? What prevents employee attrition, better pay or better management?"

Their massive study, conducted over a period of twenty-five years, was compiled into a book they entitled, *First, Break All the Rules.* The commonalities they found in high performing managers were that, first, they did not hesitate to break all the rules of conventional management practices, as the title of their book suggests.

Secondly, they placed a great deal of emphasis on the care, well-being and development of their employees. The third, Buckingham and Coffman concluded, is that employers should have a close relationship and are liked by their employees. The authors concluded:

"In today's tight labor markets, companies compete to find and keep the best employees, using pay, benefits, promotions, and training. But these well-intentioned efforts often miss the mark. The front-line manager is the key to attracting and retaining talented employees. No matter how generous its pay or how renowned its training, the company that lacks great front-line managers will suffer."

The two authors further explained how the best managers select employees based on talent, as opposed to skills or experience. They set clear expectations and define the right outcomes rather than the right steps or process to follow. They motivate people and build on each person's unique strengths rather than trying to fix their weaknesses. And, finally, they find the right fit for each person, as opposed to believing that promotion to management is automatically presumed to be the next rung on the organizational ladder.

Citing both corporate and individual performance metrics, Buckingham and Coffman concluded that the top performing companies all excelled at employee engagement and invest in their workforce. They say that an employee's commitment to his or her work comes down to basic questions, such as, "Do I know what is expected of me at work?" or, "Do my opinions count?"

One final person we interviewed on the subject of engagement was Kevin Kruse. He is another popular spokesperson on the subject, and also the author of multiple books on the topic. One of his books is simply titled *Employee Engagement*. In a recent interview, he distilled the test for employers who want to assess their employees' commitment to their work to four questions, using the acronym G.R.E.A.T.

Those questions are:

1. Growth – *Do my employees feel they are growing in their work?*
2. Recognition – *Are they being recognized for their work?*
3. Trust – *Do they trust that they and the company are on the right track?*
4. Communication – *The means by which to engage in those discussions.*

Kruse cited a number of simple, inexpensive examples of how to engage employees in these questions. He emphasized catching employees in laudable or even coachable moments to cite their behavior and let them know they are valued. He emphasized that employee engagement is neither expensive nor time consuming.

Using those four questions, are you or your employees actively engaged in their work? If no, then what can be done to engage the ambivalent, or the actively disengaged? Sheridan offered a sampling of three actions that could be taken:

1. *Volunteer them for assignments or committees.*
2. *Mix them with workers that are actively engaged.*
3. *He or she may be in the wrong job. Consider moving them into a role more suitable to their skill set.*

At the core of it all, from each of the experts we consulted, is the premise of being aware of your employees' perceptions of their work, and finding ways to align the two.

Conclusion

Well, the first thing we learned is that perception has *everything* to do with employee engagement. Whether it's our perception of the benefits we'll derive from our work, or how much we like how our boss treats us, or whether it's how much we like our co-workers and the environment, it is all based on our perceptions.

The second thing we learned goes back to the expression, "Little things mean a lot." It is the slightest occurrence that can alter our perceptions about our co-workers or the workplace, which in turn can affect our level of engagement. Consider the employee who has been diligent and effective at his or her work and was next in line for the promotion that went to someone else … someone more junior and not regarded as particularly effective at their work.

Or inversely, the boss who says, "You know things are tight right now and a raise is out of the question. But I want to thank you for the long hours you've put in to help us get this project done. Here's a gift certificate for you and your wife to go to dinner."

The behaviors and activities that surround us in our workplace are continuously shaping and reshaping our perceptions. What we choose to do or not do with those perceptions is up to us.

Chapter Fourteen
Perception and Leadership

> *If your actions inspire others to dream more, learn more, do more and become more, you are a leader.*
>
> *John Quincy Adams*

Introduction

Invariably, the discussion of perception, especially in a business or management context, seems to always lead to the question, "Do our perceptions make us better? As an employee ... or as a leader? And if so, how?"

Those are legitimate questions, and to address them, we restated the questions, as follows: "Is there a correlation between perception and leadership? And if so, how do our perceptions impact our leadership?"

The answer to the first part is, "Absolutely!"

The answer to the second part is, "Both!"

To fully address the questions in the context of leadership, we had to look at perception from both sides ... there are the perceptions leaders have of themselves; and there are the perceptions that employees have of their leaders. Those can be two entirely different perceptions. In addition, there are perceptions that can get in the way of being an effective leader.

So, where do we begin? How about with the first question, "What is the relationship between perception and leadership?"

There are numerous ways effective leaders use and don't use their perceptive abilities. Let's explore a few.

Leaders *Really* Pay Attention

According to the Mendoza College of Business at the University of Notre Dame, there are nine key qualities that effective leaders possess. They tend to be more perceptive or more observant. Better managers ask more questions, and genuinely listen to the answers. Beyond listening to the words, they tend to observe the body language of the person who's giving the answer, looking for congruence between what is being said and what the body is saying.

They tend to be able to "sense" things ... not just with individuals, but on a broader scale. They are more in tune with the company, with the marketplace, with the competition. They are more in tune with industry trends ... what's going up, what's going down, and what's going on in their industry.

Effective leaders are more perceptive about their employees ... how they are doing, who's performing, and who's not. They are more emotionally intelligent. They can sense moods. They can perceive who is distracted, who is fully engaged, who is on board, and who is not. Sometimes, their employees think they have some type of ESP or some other extraordinary sensing abilities. It turns out that they just pay closer attention.

Among the many qualities that separate great leaders from their peers, certainly one is how they use their perceptive abilities to pay attention. They observe more closely. They listen more closely. And they decipher congruencies and incongruencies more effectively, as a result. It is these finely tuned perceptions that guide them in terms of how to maneuver, how to compete, and how to lead.

In short, as we wrote in our introduction, our perceptions

are our compass. And the compasses of effective leaders seem to be more finely tuned and calibrated than others.

Conversely, ineffective leaders tend to do just the opposite. They tend to have blind spots when it comes to paying attention, even when it comes to seeing the strengths of their own team. Christine Chartrand, a human resource professional who specializes in developing assessment instruments to measure employee and leadership potential, says many aspiring or poor leaders simply do not pay close attention to the day-to-day behaviors of their teams.

That failure to observe results in a failure to leverage their most important commodity. She says, "A leader who fails to seek out the strengths of their workforce is like leading with blinders on."

Perhaps, she suggests, their focus is elsewhere. Whether they are pre-occupied with themselves or on their superiors, they are missing the most crucial part of their role as leaders. "Failing to see their team's abilities and characteristics is like only seeing the tip of the iceberg," Chartrand says.

They Suspend Beliefs

There are times when perception gets in the way of good leadership. Most leaders got to where they are because of their past successes. When a certain action results in success, the tendency is to believe that would be the correct action to take if that situation presents itself again. Leaders tend to cultivate beliefs, sometimes strong beliefs, about the right way to proceed. That is another form of bias, which may or may not be true.

Just because something worked once doesn't mean it will work again. That is one-way perceptions can get in the way of effective leadership.

Things change and so do effective leaders. Therein lies the difference between leadership and *effective* leadership.

Effective leaders are able to put their perceptions aside when they're listening to others' opinions, especially opposing points of view. In an article he published in *Inc. Magazine,* Andrew Thomas, founder and CEO of Skybell Video Doorbell, said, "Effective leaders welcome beliefs contrary to their own . . . . They realize the value of questioning widely held assumptions and biases and testing the beliefs of those around them, as well as their own."

This is one situation where the perceptive skills of talking and biases should take a back seat to the perceptive ability to listen to others. "Effective leaders listen attentively to positions that don't necessarily align with their own, and ask questions to gain a broader perspective, even knowing the answers conflict with their own opinions." They are driven, not by their ego, Thomas tells us, but by a relentless pursuit of truth seeking.

They Are Agile

That ability to listen to conflicting viewpoints leads to yet another way effective leaders distinguish themselves. According to John Spence, that ability to suspend their own beliefs and listen to others leads to another critical skill of effective leaders: they are able to change when the situation warrants. Spence is considered one of the world's top leadership development experts. He was named by the American Management Association as one of America's Top 50 Leaders to Watch, and is the author of the book, *Awesomely Simple: Essential Business Strategies for Turning Ideas Into Action.*

That ability to shift directions when the situation warrants, or be agile, according to Spence, means, "Whatever your perceptions are regarding your situation, don't hold to them too tightly. Chances are, they'll be different soon."

In his TED Talk, Spence said, "I realized that all throughout our lives, from kindergarten all the way through graduate school, doctorate and everything, we're taught to find the one right answer. If you want to pass the test, there's only one right answer. The problem is, when you graduate, there is no such thing as just one right answer. There are multiple right answers . . . . If you're not agile and adaptable and able to embrace new ideas and discard all the ideas and change your frame of reference, there is no way, in my opinion, you will be successful in the next decade."

Authors and former executives Ashok Shah and G. Ross Kelly agree. In their recently published book, *Achieving Lifetime Employability,* the authors said in a recent interview, "Given the continuous changes that are being driven by new technologies and global competition, companies are continually changing, adapting and innovating to keep up. Whatever business rules and processes were in existence last month will most likely be different next month. Employees, just like their companies, have to continually change to stay abreast."

They Speak in Specifics

In John Spence's book, *Awesomely Simple,* he described numerous ways in which effective leaders stand out. In addition to their perception skills, he says, they communicate in concrete terms … especially in setting goals.

Instead of saying, "You've got to sell more," he says, be more specific, even binary. "Your goal is to sell $2 million by the end of the month." If we get to the end of the month, he says, and you've only sold $1.7 million, the proper response is, "You're $300,000 short. How can we fix that together?"

Spence cites this as one area in which perceptions can lead us astray. From his own experiences, he says that we are all capable of perceiving ambiguously stated goals differently.

With specific, binary goals, Spence says, there's no opinion; there's no thinking; it's just data. You did it or you didn't.

They Share Accountability

Leadership in the workplace can become competitive, even combative, especially between leaders and their employees. Invariably, that can lead to teams and their leaders going in two different directions. Dileep Srinivasan, founding partner and CEO of PowerFluence, and a third contributing author to *Achieving Lifetime Employability*, says that is a sure sign of weak leadership.

Instead of scenarios where the leader says, "Here is your goal," which can result in a chasm between the leader and the team, effective leaders say, "This is our goal. How can we achieve it?" Communicating in terms of "we" versus "I" is the difference between good leaders and bad ones. Employees know in an instant, Srinivasan says, when leaders remove or separate themselves from the firing line. The moment that perception exists within the team is the moment that leader has lost all credibility.

Michael Hyatt is the founder and CEO of Michael Hyatt & Company, a leadership development firm, and author of multiple books on leadership, including *Living Forward* and *Platform*. Citing former U.S. president Harry Truman and the plate on his desk that read simply, "The Buck Stops Here," Hyatt says, "First and foremost, shared accountability means that you accept responsibility for the outcomes expected of you and the team, both good and bad. You don't blame your team; you don't blame others. And you don't blame the external environment. There are always things you could have done, or still can do to change the outcome."

"Until you take responsibility, you are a *victim*," Hyatt says. "And being a victim is the exact opposite of being a leader. Victims are passive. They are acted upon. Leaders are active. They take initiative to influence the outcome."

A sign of a good leader is when they and their entire team embrace one goal, one direction, one plan.

They Are Not Afraid to Fail

In our chapter on failure, we wrote of the many limitations people experience when they allow their fear of failure to govern their actions. More specifically, it is typically the fear of the perceived consequences of those failings. "People will think I'm stupid." Or "I may not get the promotion." Or, "What if we make a mistake?" Leaders who fail to act because of their fears, not only hold themselves back; they can hold back an entire team.

Lolly Daskal, the founder of Lead from Within and author of *The Lea*dership Gap: What Gets Between You and Your Greatness? spoke of this at length in a recent interview we conducted with her. In essence, she said, many leaders are afraid of being discovered that they don't know what everyone thinks they know.

Effective leaders, says Joel Goldstein, a leadership consultant, are not afraid to take risks. They realize, like every one of us, that failure is always a possibility. But they do not let that possibility deter them from acting. Instead, they prepare their team with contingency plans: "If this happens, then we do this."

Goldstein says the very definition of leadership "is about redefining things, finding new solutions and leading others to bigger and better things." Effective leaders don't conduct their activities while hiding behind a box or from within their office. "Leadership," he says, "is about bringing progress and provoking evolution, and none of this can be done from inside the margins of the status quo."

Remarkably good leaders, the consultant says, "stand and speak up in the face of adversity and stand up for what is right, not what is popular."

Effective leaders not only stand for themselves, but for their entire team.

Conclusion

S o, it appears that there are ways effective leaders use their perceptive powers, and ways that they put their perceptions, especially their biases, in their pockets. What we see, what we know, what we sense, how we respond, and how we inspire, are all pivotal in our quest to be effective as leaders, and all dependent on our perceptions. Allowing others to see things from their vantage point, versus our own, also is dependent on our perceptions.

Study after study cite how effective leaders "see things" that others do not. They sense when and when not to act, and what actions to take. Finely tuned perceptions, from business savvy to emotional intelligence, set leaders apart from others. They seem to see what's coming around the bend before it arrives. They seem to hear elements of key conversations that others ignore. They tend to envision solutions that others cannot see.

Those same studies cite how effective leaders use that same business savvy and emotional intelligence to know when not to speak, but to listen.

It is their perceptive abilities which guide their instincts on when to do what. It is those perceptive abilities which, in turn, guide their actions, which make them effective leaders.

Are these learned behaviors? Again, the answer is "Absolutely." That is the focus of Part III.

Part III

Managing
Our Perceptions

Chapter Fifteen
Introduction to EPIC

Every human has four endowments - self-awareness, conscience, independent will and creative imagination. These give us the ultimate human freedom... The power to choose, to respond, to change.

Stephen R. Covey

Introduction

While multiple publications address the topic of perception, and even more speak to the many challenges and approaches to effective leadership, we could find none that examine how the two impact one another in any comprehensive fashion. We know our perceptions are the radar that guides our behavior. And we know that as we enter into more global and multi-cultural interactions, we will encounter perceptions that differ from our own. Thirdly, we know that how we manage that array of perceptions will either enhance or derail our effectiveness.

Which brought us here.

In Part I, we reviewed the major factors that are the foundation of our perceptions, such as our culture, our spirituality, and even our gender. Those and other factors are the ingredients that influence what we believe and why we believe it.

In Part II, we examined how those factors can impact our interactions with others, and the implications of those interactions, both positive and negative. In many instances, our perceptions are so ingrained in our behaviors that we give little or no thought to what is driving how we engage others. In a global, multi-cultural environment, our effectiveness is totally dependent on a heightened awareness of our own interactions and an increased sensitivity to those of others.

In Part III, we intend to propose a new way to think about your perceptions … one that offers you that heightened awareness of those encounters. Think of it as a memory jog to help raise your consciousness level, or a mental framework to help you look before you leap into the situations you encounter in social settings or in the workplace. Our analysis of this approach has shown it to provide a means of being more effective in your interactions with others, more creative, more engaging, and a more effective leader.

In subsequent chapters, we will then introduce you to a collection of companion tools, including a new assessment instrument, to help further reinforce and support this new approach.

From its inception, this project has been driven by the belief that, in this new information economy, we must fundamentally reshape the lens through which we perceive, and, in turn, how others perceive us. Given the many skills, attributes and qualities we develop as employees and as leaders, research has shown that none will have the desired effect if we don't have our perceptions right.

As a point of comparison, for example, critical thinking is described as being the conscious act of thinking in a disciplined, methodical thought process. Yet our perceptions seem largely unconscious, which can be guided by a variety of factors, some known and some unknown. The results can be unpredictable, and in some cases, unfortunate. Our challenge and our objective has been to establish a method from which to train our perceptions to be the same as our critical thinking: more thoughtful, more disciplined, more methodical.

What we see and hear, and how we interpret what we see and hear, are the foundation that drives our beliefs, which in turn, drive our behaviors. Both consciously and unconsciously, our perceptions must be more in-tune and more responsive to this emerging multi-cultural world in which we are now living. This book, and its companion tools, are intended to serve as a foundation in which to do just that.

So, what is this new approach to aid us in how we better manage our perceptions?

E.P.I.C.

In the research and analysis phase of this project, we interviewed business leaders, entrepreneurs, self-made millionaires, coaches, consultants, academicians, and industry leaders. As we have chronicled in previous chapters, they all speak to how our perceptions drive our behavior, and how they can drive us in the right direction, or the wrong one. Our interviewees consistently cited the factors that shape and influence our perceptions, such as our culture, gender, spirituality, etc. They were also remarkably consistent in citing the impact of our perceptions in guiding our behaviors and attributes, such as critical thinking, creativity, and collaboration.

Where our experts varied in their thinking, however, is when we got into the questions of how do we, in a more conscientious and effective way, better monitor and guide our perceptions? How do we harness the power of our perceptions to take our performance to the next level … the next level of collaboration, engagement, creativity, and leadership, etc.?

Our experts' answers were all insightful and valid. But the sheer volume and variety of those answers made our challenge even more difficult. We were left with an embarrassment of riches. How could we distill all that we heard into a digestible, memorable and useful synopsis?

Our examination took us to the game of golf.

When a golfer is preparing to hit their next shot, there are probably fifty-plus things he or she must do correctly to execute a good shot. How is it that good golfers seemingly execute flawlessly, while lesser golfers seem to nervously stand over their shots, while reminding themselves of all the key elements they must execute to hit their shot correctly … just before slicing their ball into the woods?

Knowing their students try to remember too much information, which invariably leads to them hitting bad shots, golf instructors try to help their students reduce those fifty "swing thoughts" down to five. Then down to three, or one. And eventually, none! With enough practice and repetition, those swing thoughts become second nature.

That was our challenge. What are the swing thoughts of perception? Given all we learned from our experts, and all that our research uncovered, what were the common themes, the patterns? How could we compile everything we learned about perception into nice, convenient, bite-sized chunks, and still maintain the integrity and the comprehensive nature of this complex subject?

Themes began to emerge.

One of those themes was how we must be more conscious,

more aware of our perceptions and how they might impact others. In other words, we must use our curiosity and emotional intelligence to be more in tune with our perceptions. Another of those themes was how we must be able to sort through the myriad of our perceptual intakes, and be able to anticipate or predict the possibilities of the circumstance. In other words, apply our curiosity and critical thinking to the perception process.

There were other themes, but collectively, they all translated into the need to apply the technique of problem solving to our perceptions. You know, analyze the situation, consider the alternatives, factor in all of the implications of your solution, then act. In other words, look before leaping.

In the context of perception, that process looked more like the process of evaluating, predicting, interpreting, and reshaping, or *correlating* one's perceptions. That eventually took us to the acronym EPIC, which stands for:

Evaluation,

Prediction,

Interpretation, and

Correlation

EPIC came to represent the thought sequence to monitor and guide our perceptions, and make us more aware of what we're walking into, before we proceed. EPIC became our "swing thought."

Whether working with others, attempting to lead others, or whether simply reaching out to others, think of EPIC as your checklist for bringing your perceptions to a more conscious level.

The result? The more aware you are of your perceptions, the

more effectively you engage and influence others!

Let's take a look at each of its elements in a little more detail.

Chapter Sixteen
Assessing Your Perceptiveness

> *Self-assessment and attempts at self-improvement are essential aspects of leadership.*
>
> *Robert A. Burton*

Introduction

I s your perception working for you, or against you? Are you conscious of the way you're interacting with others, or, are you committing social or verbal faux paus without even knowing it?

As we have outlined in previous chapters, our perceptions are engaged on a 24/7 basis, and unless trained to do otherwise, they are operating on automatic pilot. They are taking us where they've been conditioned to go. The inputs your brain receives today and the inputs that are embedded in your subconscious can be two different things.

Do I believe the most effective leaders are white males with a touch of gray in their hair, or is that a product of long-held beliefs? Do I believe that the most innovative technologies emanate from the Silicon Valley in the United States, or is that a perception that has been propagated by the media? And, if those are my perceptions, how much credence do I give to the data that is in contrast to those beliefs? Our perceptions can take us to new levels of understanding and interactions with others, or they can unconsciously and unknowingly keep us bound by status-quo thinking, thus limiting our ability to engage, to learn, or to lead. This analysis led us to create a simplified, four-step process to become more aware of our perceptions and how to put them to more effective use in our interactions with others.

Those four steps involve (1) Evaluating our own perceptions; (2) Predicting or anticipating other's perceptions; (3) Interpreting the collective environment or scenario; and (4) Correlating or concluding the most effective approach to managing the situation.

This came to be collectively referred to as **E.P.I.C.**

E.P.I.C. was created to help remove those limitations. The more conscious and aware we are of our perceptions, and the more we understand why we perceive things the way we do, the better we will be at navigating the waters of today's diverse, multi-cultural and ever-changing environment. Yet, those mental triggers of E.P.I.C. are merely a beginning to opening ourselves to receiving new or different inputs.

As we've learned in previous academic and training endeavors, true behavioral change doesn't happen simply by reading about how we can improve. That may be necessary, but it is not sufficient. Behavioral change comes through action, and that action begins by understanding where we are; establishing a baseline, so to speak. From losing weight to learning to hit a golf ball, it all begins with stepping on the scales or getting to the driving range to determine our starting point. To pursue a future state, we must first know our current state.

Which brings us here.

This project began with a hypothesis that our perceptions are the window into what we believe and how we interact with others. If we are living and working only with others who share our beliefs, that may be OK. However, the likelihood of that being the case diminishes by the day. Our world is shrinking at an unprecedented rate. Our workplace is more global, more technical, and more diversified than ever before, and will continue on that same path.

The more we explored this topic, the more we realized its importance in how we interact in the workplace and in our everyday lives. And the deeper we got, the more we realized that merely writing about our findings was also necessary, but not sufficient. The more we spoke with business leaders, entrepreneurs and academicians from different backgrounds and different cultures, the more we wanted our readers not only to have an academic understanding of the need to improve their perceptual quotients, but also to provide them the means that would help them do so. That, we discovered, would require a companion tool to this book … an assessment instrument that allows individuals and organizations to actually facilitate change about the way in which they perceive themselves and one another.

That endeavor began by conducting an examination of the existing assessment instruments related to the topic of perception. We learned that the numbers were few, and in many ways, limiting. We also learned why that may be.

Assessment Instruments on Perception

In order to assess something, we must first define what we are measuring. And in the case of perception, that's not as simple and straightforward as it may seem. Due to the pervasive nature of the topic and its sheer complexity, perception is a term that can be challenging to define, especially for measurement purposes. It's one thing to talk about the subject in general terms. It is another thing altogether when you get into the arena of quantifying the topic.

It is from that perspective that we embarked on a review of the existing survey instruments on the topic of perception. Consider the following existing instruments that measure perception:

• *The Employee Perception Scale,* or EPS can be an effective instrument in measuring items such as confidence, trust, interest, teaching, problem solving, communicating, opinion seeking, and accomplishments. However, with our focus being more specifically on the diverse or multi-cultural work environment, we continued our review.

• Another instrument, the *Performance Environment Perception Scale,* or PEPS was given its most extensive review in Australia, where it was found to effectively establish the relationship between the work environment and performance.

Many of the existing instruments designed to assess how one perceives, we found, often overlook the critical elements of IQ, for intellectual intelligence, EQ for emotional intelligence, combined with what has been labeled as CQ for cultural intelligence.

Collectively, those are critical ingredients for what is now known as PQ, for *perceptual quotient.* One's perceptional intelligence combines aspects of all these areas. By employing these elements together, you avoid the issues of cultural or ethnic stereotyping to be open to recognizing the individual, and not their background or heritage. Eliminating bias in the workplace means receiving better ideas, a wider perspective, and the foundation from which to better compete in the global marketplace.

Do you have strong beliefs, or are you open to new thoughts or ideas? Do you believe it because that's what you've been taught to believe? Or is it something you really believe?

Given the limitations of the existing instruments on the market, we were compelled to create our own. Our objective was to develop a scientifically validated instrument that could be used both by individuals and organizations to assess their perceptual abilities and limitations within today's complex environment.

Fortunately, one of our co-authors, Dr. Diane Hamilton, had the expertise we needed for such an effort. She led the development of a similar instrument on the related topic of curiosity. Besides hosting a nationally syndicated radio program on the topic of leadership, Dr. Hamilton is perhaps best known in corporate and workplace circles for having created the *Curiosity Code Index®*. The CCI has been employed by individuals and organizations to assess and increase their curiosity. That instrument, employers have found, can translate to improvements in the areas of creativity, employee engagement and leadership, among other factors.

Our intent was to develop a similar instrument that would measure one's perception in a diverse environment. Like our curiosity, our perceptions play a large role in issues such as employee engagement, leadership and innovation. And like the CCI which measures one's curiosity, our goal was to create a comparable instrument that provides insights and guidance on our perceptions.

With those objectives, Dr. Hamilton and her team went to work. After formulating the E.P.I.C. model, she used factor analysis to formulate the questions which would result in the instrument being a valid tool for determining factors involved in perception in the workplace.

The result of the effort is called *The Perception Power Index, or PPI.*

Consciously or unconsciously, the brain is processing these thoughts at lightning speed. So, what are the critical skills embedded in this process, and how does the PPI assess them?

We have written about the importance of traits such as openness, curiosity, emotional intelligence, and empathy when confronted with different situations. The PPI is constructed and validated to examine these and all the other factors that impact our perceptions.

The Perception Power Index (PPI)\

The Perception Power Index (PPI) measures the proposed four factors involved in the perception process: Evaluation, Prediction, Interpretation, and Correlation. As in her previous assessment on curiosity, the validity of the PPI was evaluated using both exploratory and confirmatory factor analyses.

The Perception Power Index (PPI) addresses the critical attributes of emotional intelligence in terms of how we understand or perceive our emotions and those of others. It further examines the intellectual and reasoning capabilities associated with IQ and critical thinking, and the dimensions associated with our curiosity and cultural quotients, (CQ1) and (CQ2).

With those components of EQ, IQ, CQ1 and CQ2 as its foundation, the PPI further examines how our gender impacts our perceptions.

Additionally, the PPI explores one's ability to remain cognizant of those factors while confronted with different situational variables, when confronted with factors such as stress or emotional discomfort.

When interacting with individuals who trigger certain responses within us, it is important to recognize that reaction. While all of us experience emotions in the communication process, it is the successful individuals who are in tune with those emotions.

Awareness of those emotions is essential. Having control of those emotions is even more so. The PPI is also designed to examine your self-control. How well are you able to demonstrate the proper restraint to explore the situation further, before reacting?

How well are you able to assess multiple inter- and intrapersonal variables all at once in business or social circumstances with another individual? What about with two other individuals? What about three, four, five, or seven? And all from various backgrounds and cultures? Will they see the situation the same as you?

Making assumptions and conclusions about a situation is one thing. Making *educated* assumptions, in real time, is another altogether.

Assuming you are able to discern and predict differences in a multi-cultural and diverse setting, how open are you to incorporating those differences into your actions? Openness is a byproduct of our curiosity.

When we're curious, we ask questions, which can lead to

better understanding of the situation. On the other hand, the absence of being open can be impacted by fear, assumptions (the voice in our head), technology, and environment. Are you prone to emotional reaction or judgments in those circumstances? Or, are you more open to learning more?

When we work on developing our question-asking skills and recognize that we can interact better with others when we do that, we can truly experience the power of curiosity and openness to other's perspectives.

Using logic in a situation can help overcome some of the issues that evolve from being overly influenced by those emotions. Logic requires reasoning ... looking for connections between things. Researching facts and exploring multiple reliable sources to verify those facts can be critical.

Finally, how well are you able to integrate this myriad of factors into your behaviors?

The Perception Power Index not only examines these questions, but the various traits that impact these behaviors; traits such as our intellectual quotient, emotional intelligence, curiosity, cultural intelligence, and others that are the collective drivers and determinants of our perceptual quotient.

Conclusion

The previously existing instruments designed to assess how one perceives have often overlooked the critical elements of intellectual intelligence, emotional intelligence, curiosity intelligence, and what is referred to as cultural intelligence.

Our intellectual quotient (IQ) gives us an idea of our cognitive ability compared to the general population. It scores our ability to solve problems, reason, and recognize relationships. The IQ test is more about how well you understand things rather than the quantity of how much you know. That is one of the reasons that the score does not change much. IQ tests also do not measure things like creativity, wisdom, and other aspects of intelligence; however, the assessment can give a good indication of intellectual abilities and potential.

Our emotional quotient (EQ) is based on how well we recognize our emotions and those in others and adjust our behavior accordingly. Although many have studied it, emotional intelligence was made popular by the work of Daniel Goleman. Goleman found four factors associated with EI, including Self-Awareness, Self-Management, Social Awareness, and Relationship Management. The good news about emotional intelligence is that it can be improved and developed.

Our curiosity quotient (CQ1) is a measure of our interest and enthusiasm to explore new and different ideas, which is essential in understanding our own and others' perspectives. It is equally important in our exploration and development of strategies and action plans to create an open-minded way of interacting with others.

Our cultural quotient (CQ2) is based on our capability to relate and work effectively across cultures. This can be impacted by our curiosity to learn more about other people. It includes our ability to recognize things that others do that might seem ambiguous to us, but have significant meaning to them. It involves understanding other people's decisions that might be impacted by their belief system, attitudes, and values. It can include recognizing body language, visual cues, auditory cues, and not relying on stereotypes.

These traits and characteristics collectively are the critical ingredients for what is now known as our PQ, our perceptual quotient. However, each of these ingredients play multiple and different roles in each phase of the E.P.I.C. process. Recognizing this, the PPI instrument was created and validated to assess this complex mapping of skills and E.P.I.C. segments.

Every employee in every organization brings a different set of perceptions and biases with them. Left unattended, those biases can create divisions, factions and barriers, which impact cooperation, teamwork and all the ingredients essential to productivity and employee engagement.

The E.P.I.C. process and its companion Perception Power Index (PPI) assessment instrument are not intended to eliminate those differences, but to encourage and enable a better understanding of those differences. As many studies have shown, diversity in the workplace is an invaluable asset. Critical to leveraging that asset is embracing that diversity.

How do you or your organization rank in terms of the E.P.I.C. process?

Chapter Seventeen
Evaluation

> *Wisdom is the awareness and acknowledgement of the gap between life as you perceive, project and wish it to be and life as it is.*
>
> *Rasheed Ogunlaru*

Evaluation

The evaluation component of EPIC is, in essence, being aware of the situation, and in particular, of your own beliefs and values that you bring to the situation. To evaluate, as we discussed, is to question, to examine, to assess. It is to apply your emotional intelligence primarily to examine your own perceptions about the situation. Do you have strong beliefs regarding the situation? Are you open to new thoughts or ideas? Do you believe it because that's what you've been taught to believe? Or is it something you *really* believe?

Consciously or unconsciously, the brain is processing these thoughts at lightning speed. So, what are the critical skills embedded in this process?

Self-awareness is a critical component of emotional intelligence. When interacting with individuals who trigger certain responses within us, it is important to recognize that reaction. While all of us experience emotions in the communication process, it is the successful individuals who are in tune with those emotions.

Awareness of those emotions is essential. Having control of those emotions is even more so. The PPI is also designed to examine your self-control. How well are you able to demonstrate the proper restraint to explore the situation further, before reacting?

David Grossman wrote in T*he Cost of Poor Communications* that in a survey of 400 companies with 100,000+ employees, poor communication with their employees, including skills such as empathy, curiosity and emotional intelligence, cost their company in excess of $60 million per year. Emotional intelligence is described as recognizing our own emotions, and the emotions of others, in one's interactions.

Evaluation in EPIC is applying that first element of emotional intelligence and knowing our own emotions going into a situation, or self-assessment! How we communicate with others in a business situation can elevate us, or can be the kiss of death. Whether we realize it or not, others are assessing us in terms of what we say and how we say it. That self-assessment is the cornerstone to managing any social or business interaction.

Earlier in her career, Diane Hamilton worked for a pharmaceutical organization that placed a heavy premium on how its employees interacted with customers, and rated and compensated its employees accordingly. Long before theories of emotional intelligence had become well-known, this organization was already training and assessing their sales professionals on their self-awareness.

Effective communication skills have proven to be far more than being in tune with others or being nice. It has a direct impact on the employees and company's performance. In contrast, conversational exchanges which include conflict, sarcasm, misconceptions, and other perception-related issues not only cause breakdowns in communication, they have a direct impact on a company's revenues and profits.

What was unique about this pharmaceutical company's evaluation and training process was its focus on the importance of recognizing how employees communicate, including situational drills in self-control, stress management, body language, tone of voice, and even non-verbal and verbal messaging related to gender. Employees' performance in those areas were essential to their careers in the company. That focus on self-awareness and communications was deemed to be instrumental in the company being the 5th highest-ranked pharmaceutical company in the world.

So, what are some of the behavioral situations that challenge our perception and how might we combat them?

The most direct, and perhaps the most challenging aspect of our ability to evaluate a perceptual circumstance is our routine face-to-face interactions. Others' viewpoints, tone of voice, accents or any other dimension of their speech, can provoke immediate judgments. It can be challenging to keep our composure when communicating with people who might not share our viewpoints or speak with a foreign accent. Self-awareness is an important component of emotional intelligence. When interacting with individuals who provoke some type of emotional reaction, it is important to be aware of our feelings and resist the urge to let our emotions lead our interactions. Taking time to reflect on what caused the emotional reaction can be critical for proper communication.

That brings up a second challenge: self-control. It's one thing to be aware of our emotions. It's another thing to refrain from acting on them. Some form of emotion, be it intense anger or mild amusement, is present in virtually every human interaction. How we respond to or keep those emotions in check is challenging but crucial.

Differences of opinion can lead to a debate. Debates can lead to arguing. Arguing can lead to anger. Anger can lead to regretful outbursts. We've all been there. That is an unfortunate, but all-too-common experience. Yelling and name-calling are ineffective and even destructive in the workplace, and the individual who resorts to that type of response is an ineffective contributor, especially in a challenging circumstance, such as a crisis situation.

The recent coronavirus is a classic example. What were your thoughts as you listened to the health care professionals and the politicians debate the virtues of closing everything down vs. the impact on the economy? Two major aspects of our existence–the economy and our health–pitted against one another. How emotional were you in listening to those debates? Or, while participating in those debates?

Our ability to recognize when our emotions are interfering with our communication, and controlling those emotions, is essential. Taking deep breaths and pausing to cool down before making any decisions or interacting with others in inappropriate ways is a first step in maintaining self-control.

An accompanying byproduct of the lack of self-control is stress. We all experience stress. Some even thrive on it. But stress is the enemy of effective interactions. Mindfulness has become a useful technique to keep cool heads in times of stress. Coming up with a routine where calming techniques are practiced can be a very important part of dealing with daily stresses.

Recognizing that we are all susceptible to saying inappropriate or harmful things in the heat of the moment, there is another invaluable trait in evaluating perceptions effectively: the simple humane act of forgiveness.

Sometimes we misinterpret what others mean in our conversations. Sometimes we don't like what they said, or even how they said it. Minor misperceptions can lead to grudges. In these situations, the power of forgiveness can be very impactful. We are all human beings who make mistakes. Holding on to negative emotions often hurts us more than it hurts other people. It can be helpful to open lines of communication with those with whom you have had disagreements to ensure future negative situations do not occur.

Other dynamics that can affect our ability to effectively evaluate a situation and communicate are seemingly minor issues like body language, or tone of voice, or even the gender or nationality of the other party.

Our non-verbal communication, or body language, is a very significant component of our communication process, and can be interpreted differently based on cultural or situational issues. It is critical to recognize the meaning we assign to body language. What we might perceive as something innocent could be taken differently by someone from another culture. When in doubt, it is important to do research to determine the proper etiquette.

Similarly, tone of voice is an essential element of our verbal communication, and positively or negatively, tone can evoke our emotional reactions. We can perceive someone with a soft voice as timid, or the opposite of those that project a loud, booming voice.

We can even infer a tone in our written communications. Words or sentences written in ALL CAPS or in "quotation marks," can infer a certain attitude or opinion.

Additionally, someone's gender or nationality can cause

subtle, but significant challenges to our ability to evaluate our interactions. Men communicate with other men differently than with women. Social scientists have long talked about the "codes" that men and women use when communicating with others of their own agenda.

Communicating in diverse settings of genders and nationalities are, by definition, more complex and offer far more opportunities to misperceive or react emotionally.

Our ability to be aware of our own emotions and how we express those emotions, both verbally and non-verbally, are the linchpin to evaluating any social interaction in which our perceptions play a large role. And it is for that reason that the E in EPIC is to Evaluate and understand our emotions before we engage in those communications.

Chapter Eighteen
Prediction

Every living creature on this planet has a conscious subjective perspective of the world.

Abhijit Naskar

Prediction

The second element of the EPIC process is Prediction. After evaluating or establishing an awareness of your own perceptions, questions follow. How do others perceive the situation? What is the other party's view of the situation? Are they of similar or differing beliefs? If Evaluation is about self-awareness, Prediction is about awareness of others and the situation. To predict is to draw educated conclusions and assumptions about the situation and the people you are about to engage. It is as if to say, "I know how I feel about the situation. But how will others feel about the situation?"

Will others see the situation the same as you, or differently? We hear about the importance of emotional intelligence, especially empathy in many different situations and parts of our perception process. When evaluating situations, if we intend to influence others, it is critical that we adjust our communication style to meet other people's needs for how they prefer to interact.

Additionally, we must explore our awareness and ability to recognize when people are distracted by outside circumstances or overcome by stress. When others act in a way that seems out of character, is your tendency to judge or criticize, or do you empathize?

Prediction is our ability to draw conclusions about others' point of view. Whereas the "E" component places an emphasis on self-awareness, the "P" component is about one's awareness of others' viewpoints and perceptions.

As previously discussed, making assumptions about alternative viewpoints is one thing. Making *educated* assumptions about how others view a particular situation is another. To predict is to look beyond your own perceptions, biases and beliefs, to those around you. It is not just to make assumptions, but to make educated assumptions.

Whereas Evaluate is to assess our own emotions, Prediction is to assess, understand and predict how the other participant or participants in our encounters with others might respond in a given situation. This, too, is an aspect of emotional intelligence in which empathy and using our curiosity are the essential skills. Those are skills that are emerging as more and more essential in the workplace, especially given the increasing diversity of the workforce, yet found to be sorely lacking.

To assess our Prediction capabilities, we must (a) assess our abilities to understand other views or perceptions regarding a situation or circumstance; and (b) identify any potential obstacles or factors that may inhibit that ability.

A recent research study found that people avoid empathy because of the mental effort required. A Workplace Empathy Monitor report found that 80 percent of employees believe the current state of empathy in U.S. organizations requires significant improvement.

To make effective decisions and interact appropriately with others, the study tells us, we must be able to empathize and consider alternative viewpoints. Only then can we make predictions about potential outcomes.

This is borne out in many companies, especially those that place a heavy premium on service, such as airlines. Consider the case of Ryanair. After witnessing a string of blunders by other airlines, such as United, Ryanair decided to implement a program it called, "Always Getting Better," which focused on issues they concluded were annoying to air travelers, such as hidden charges, unallocated seating, and carry-on baggage restrictions.

By making these predictions and making changes in these areas, the company increased their net profit by $1.39 billion. CEO Michael O'Leary famously remarked, "If I'd only known being nice to customers was going to work so well, I'd have started many years ago." Their success led to their being listed as one of the most empathetic companies in a report by *HBR*.

Simply put, predicting people's needs allows us to understand their emotions and their intentions and desires. That understanding is the foundation for determining more creative alternatives in how to approach a situation or solve problems.

Empathy and curiosity are essential components to understanding, anticipating, and predicting what customers need and adjusting our behaviors accordingly. Just asking questions is not enough. Just as an introvert prefers to communicate differently from an extrovert, there are a wealth of factors that influence other people's needs, desires, and decisions. Our ability to predict is what turns casual customers into loyal followers.

Just as the Evaluation in E.P.I.C. is about being in tune with our own emotions, Prediction is about having that same awareness of the emotions of others. That, again, shines the spotlight on our emotional intelligence, and more specifically, our ability to empathize. When evaluating situations, it is critical that we adjust our communication style to meet other people's needs for how they prefer to interact.

The ability to evaluate requires empathy. And empathy brings with it many characteristics and traits, all of which are equally essential. Among those is sensitivity. Sometimes we might not understand why someone feels or acts a certain way, but it is critical to be sensitive to the possibility that their behavior is being driven by stress or some other factor. When others act in a way that seems out of character, it is essential to consider what emotional situation or stress might have impacted them.

Another of those qualities is acceptance. There is a very human desire in each of us to be accepted. The sheer act of suspending judgment and accepting the situation can go a long way to a better understanding of a situation.

It would be easy for us to make judgments of other's communications; what is good, what is bad, or what is or is not acceptable based on our own ethics and cultural upbringing. What might seem like an unthinkable thing to do in our culture might seem traditional in another. Avoiding placing our values on others is critical. What we might see as an inaccuracy or uncomfortable situation usually stems from our past exposure to that situation and the importance we have assigned to it.

Tony Alessandra, author, motivational speaker and founder of Assessments24x7 suggested we take the Golden Rule one step further to a "Platinum Rule": *Treat others as they would want to be treated!*

Beyond our ability to empathize and to predict the behaviors of others is our ability to apply our critical thinking skills.

Whether we engage in some type of formal research or

spontaneously consider a variety of alternatives to the situation, that exploration is essential.

Our willingness to resist drawing conclusions without facts, and to apply all of the elements of our critical thinking skills to the situation, gives us a broader and more accurate assessment of how we perceive others.

Chapter Nineteen
Interpretation

> *Wisdom comes from knowing that what others say about you is not your reality. It's their reality.*
>
> *Kristin Michelle Elizabeth*

Interpretation

The third element of the **EPIC** process is to **Interpret**.
Leveraging your emotional intelligence and critical thinking skills
to navigate the *evaluation* and *prediction* steps, you understand
how you perceive the situation, and have concluded how others
might perceive the situation. *Interpretation* is about integrating
the two to determine how you should proceed. Your capabilities
in this area are assessed by your openness, understanding, and
logic in drawing conclusions.

Openness, or open-minded thinking, often comes from
being curious. Asking questions leads to better understanding.
Curiosity can be impacted by fear, assumptions (the voice in
our head), technology, and environment. When we work on
developing our question-asking skills and recognize that we
can interact better with others when we do that, we can truly
experience the power of curiosity and openness to others'
perspectives.

Using logic in a situation can help overcome some of the
issues that evolve from being overly influenced by emotions.
Logic requires reasoning ... looking for connections between
things. Researching facts and exploring multiple reliable sources

to verify those facts can be critical. Consider the origins of ideas. Avoid vague or ambiguous wording when sharing ideas.

Interpretation is measured by one's cultural quotient to decipher one's own beliefs and perceptions, as well as others', and to employ logical thinking to make an accurate interpretation of how to proceed, given the array of personal, political, and spiritual differences that may exist.

Evaluation and Prediction are about understanding *what* we and others bring into a dialogue or situation. Interpretation is about *why!* We learned earlier in this treatise that culture is a major influencer of behavior. A recent Global Human Capital Trends report further verified that premise, finding that culture drives people's behavior, including innovation and customer service. The report found that 82% of CEOs and HR leaders believe behavior and reward systems that take culture into account are a significant competitive advantage.

It is for that reason that leading companies are using behavioral data to manage and influence their culture to improve customer service, employee engagement, and retention. To interpret is to assess the meaning behind those behaviors. Why are certain issues important to people? Their behaviors could be driven by their religion, politics, and other personal aspects of their culture. Two individuals could have the same experience and interpret that experience in dramatically different ways.

To interpret is to understand how those differences impact their experiences, and in turn, relationships. It is the key to finding common ground, which is essential in decision making, negotiations, and conflict resolution.

One company that has shown great strides in interpreting the needs of its employees and its customers, for example, is Netflix.

Their organization's culture presentation has been downloaded and shared more than 12 million times since 2009. Their ability to interpret the needs of their employees has resulted in a generous corporate perk program with unlimited vacations, flexible work schedules, and limited supervision. It is that understanding which has yielded high levels of employee engagement and high yields in its financial performance.

Interpreting is understanding what is important to others and thus finding common ground.

Effective negotiations and interactions require us to look at things from an outside perspective. What we believe to be perks or advantages for our customers or employees might not be the same as what they believe.

We must explore the value everyone places on rewards. We must consider how growing up in a particular area, or being of a certain race or of a specific gender might influence how we interpret meaning. If we shut out options because things have never been done that way in our past, we might be just buying into status quo thinking. By using curiosity to explore possibilities with an open mind and with foresight for how it could impact the future, we can see value in everyone's insights.

The **E** and the **P** in **EPIC** are about assessing and understanding our own emotions and perceptions, and those of others, the **I** is about putting that collective data together, to Interpret that data.

Our ability to effectively interpret our and others' perceptions require us to mentally weave our way through a montage of emotions, biases and preconceived ideas about the situation at hand. Whereas this too requires us to apply our various emotional, intellectual and cultural abilities, it is those attributes combined with our critical thinking skills that provide us this ability.

The combination of openness to the ways others may be thinking and to our own logical thinking capabilities can be a challenging mix of attributes. But it is just that combination that allows us to assess the variety of thoughts and judgments that comprise a situation and make sense of it all.

It is our openness to other points of view–or even alternative facts–that gives us unfettered access to the thoughts and biases of others. It is our logic that gives us the ability to sort through those alternative viewpoints and mesh them with our own to extract an educated analysis of the situation.

It is this collection of attributes that allows us to make our way through the collection of data points, from others not being given ample consideration to their feelings, to our own emotions of not being fully recognized in a situation. It is this combination of virtues that enables us to acknowledge feelings, beliefs and points of view that we don't agree with or even acknowledge as valid.

Be it politics, religion or the very existence of other philosophies of life, our ability to invite these different viewpoints, factor them with our own, and effectively interpret the combined scenario those circumstances produce requires just that combination of attributes.

To interpret is to extract a meaningful understanding from a wildly different array of feelings, beliefs, attitudes and opinions, and be prepared to comfortably engage.

Chapter Twenty
Correlation

Through our awareness, we can open the inheritance of our qualities or talents, and behind that, reside in the stillness of being.

Georgi Y. Johnson,

Correlation

The fourth and final element in the EPIC process of monitoring and managing our perceptions, is to Correlate, to (1) take in all the sensory inputs you are receiving, both your own and from others, (2) analyze and synthesize the data with the situation and circumstances, and (3) calculate the appropriate response.

To correlate suggests you've grown smarter and have acclimated yourself to a new set of perceptions and behaviors.

Skill wise, correlation requires a combination of intelligence, emotional intelligence and cultural sensitivity to understand your own perceptions, how the perceptions of others may differ, and to make rational, sensitive, and logical conclusions as to how to proceed.

To assess our ability to correlate is to examine this array of skills and attributes, emphasizing one's own fact-finding abilities, combined with the sensitivity and sensing skills to be aware of what others may or may not know or understand. For example, does the other person not know the situation, or, are they not able to adequately discuss it due to language or cultural barriers?

Many people come to conclusions without researching facts.

Even if we have done our research, that does not mean others have done theirs. Sharing ideas with others who might not know what they do not know can be helpful. It is critical not to come across as condescending. Having an attitude of sharing rather than judgment is critical.

Further, in recognizing that others might not have done their research, it is also important to recognize they might not be familiar with all variables. Some people might not be experienced in a certain area. They might not know how to determine the nuances of a situation. If we assume everyone has gone through the same process as we have, we might have assumed incorrectly.

When we engage others effectively, we take all that we have learned from our evaluation, prediction, and interpretation to draw intelligent conclusions. Understanding ourselves, the other parties involved, the circumstances, and the real-time dynamics of the situation, correlation is a systematic examination and understanding of all the factors involved. That applies to simple interactions, business negotiations, or even choosing stocks in the stock market. For example, why would we choose to invest in companies like FedEx, ESPN, Amazon, Turner Broadcasting, or Tesla before they ever turn a profit?

Consider the story of Frederick Smith, who came up with the idea for overnight delivery in 1962 that he outlined in a paper while attending Yale. Almost ten years later, based on his original idea, in 1971 he founded Federal Express. The company failed to take off initially and wasn't profitable until 1975. What did those original shareholders see that helped him raise $11 million, and eventually, enormous profits?

Fred Smith assessed and understood the mindset of early investors, and was able to shape his presentation to those concerns.

In turn, those investors had to make a similar assessment of Fred Smith. It was not just the idea that intrigued them, but their assessment of the individual behind that idea.

This is the concluding challenge … to take in and absorb wildly different ideas from a most diverse range of people places and circumstances. There are those who bring an uneducated point of view. There are those who will judge you for the color of your skin, your culture, or even your gender. There are those who will judge you because you are affiliated or associated with the wrong organization. There are those who approach you with a deeply entrenched, unalterable point of view, unwilling to consider any thought or idea that is contrary. Or those whose viewpoints have been shaped by a lifestyle or a culture that is dramatically different from your own.

Likewise, you will encounter those whose viewpoints challenge your own. How open will you be to entertain these opposing circumstances, at a time when you can least afford to alienate? How receptive will you be?

To correlate these many factors or these various circumstances—an understanding of ourselves and others, and the myriad of situational variables we encounter in a given situation—is the sum-total of the intent of E.P.I.C. This amalgam of factors are those that have been tested and validated to equip and enable our understanding and, ultimately, our effective management of those factors and circumstances.

Armed with the proper tools and mindset, our perceptions are invaluable. They guide us in our own behaviors and enable us to embrace others of different languages, different cultures, and different points of view. E.P.I.C. provides that mindset. With that, we propose that you let your perceptions flourish … through all of your senses. Be in the moment. Taste the wine. Hear what your best friend, your manager, or even your most dreaded opponent is trying to tell you. Through it all, keep your E.P.I.C. radar turned on and finely-tuned.

Conclusion

> *Follow the evidence to where it leads, even if the conclusion is uncomfortable.*
>
> **Steven James**

S o, what have we learned here? In a nutshell, we've learned that, in working or living in a multi-cultural environment, our perceptions are either our silent enabler, or our silent inhibitor. Like breathing, or sneezing, or the hiccups, our perceptions are an involuntary reaction to the many events and situations that we confront in our daily lives, unless we develop a voluntary mechanism to become more aware of our perceptions and guide them as the situation warrants.

As we stated in the introduction to this book, this project began with a simple premise:

Our perceptions are a powerful and in many cases, subliminal forces that play a major role in shaping our attitudes, our behaviors and our interactions with others. Therefore, in order to work more effectively in a global, multi-cultural environment, a more conscious approach to being aware of, and better managing our perceptions is essential.

This book, the creation of the E.P.I.C. approach to better managing our perceptions, and the companion PPI Assessment instrument from which individuals and organizations can take the necessary actions, are the basic outputs of our work.

In an interview, we were asked what the key messages are that we would impart to readers. If you had to boil it all down, they asked, what should the reader know and do after reading this book? In response, we began with the E.P.I.C. process and the PPI assessment instrument, as summarized in the previous chapters, as key takeaways. They serve as the mechanisms from which to raise one's awareness of their perceptions, and from which to better understand how they may be perceived in a diverse, multi-cultural environment.

The rationale for taking those proposed actions are outlined in the main body of this book, but if we were to summarize our learnings, they could best be summarized as follows:

1. Our perceptions are indeed our compass.

As we suspected when we began, we learned that our perceptions, and our interpretations of their meanings, are perhaps the most powerful factor in influencing our thoughts, our beliefs and our actions. Put in the context of a multi-cultural work environment, that is perhaps even more so.

Consciously or unconsciously, it is our perceptions that are the initial trigger in determining how we respond to a given situation, or even what we believe to be the right course of action. Our beliefs, including our biases, serve as our instinctual guide to our answers, no matter the question.

2) Many of our perceptions are deeply embedded, shaped at the time when we are most impressionable, by our family, by our culture, by our faith.

Though it is true that our perceptions tend to change and become more solidified as we age, it is those most impressionable years of our youth that serve as the foundation of how we view the world. Depending on our exposure to other cultures and spiritual beliefs as we age, our earlier perceptions can either be modified or solidified as we grow older.

James Yang, a technology executive in his home country of Taiwan, found himself partnered with a large Japanese firm on a multi-million dollar project. Working with the Japanese seemed to trigger in him a great deal of emotional angst. When he shared his concerns with his boss, he told his superior the words of his father resounded loudly in his head from the time he was a little boy. His father told him, "Son, the Japanese destroyed our village in World War II. Never trust them."

What we believe and how it manifests itself can be grounded in new discoveries, or long-held, deep-seated beliefs.

3) Many of our perceptions are hidden in our subconscious, making us unaware of their origins or why we feel the way we do.

When things look odd to us, by definition, that means they are different from what we are accustomed to. Upon observing that the English people drive on the "wrong" side of the road, the American commented, "Don't they know they're supposed to be driving on the other side of the road? They can cause accidents driving like that."

Our perceptions are not what is true, but only what we know to be true.

4) Our perceptions can take us to new learnings and discoveries, or close us off from accepting and adapting to the new realities of a fast-changing world.

Depending on the circumstances, and our audience, our perceptions either enable or inhibit our abilities to work in a multi-cultural environment. While our beliefs, actions and natural tendencies may feel comfortable and right in our own environment, they can be off-putting or offensive to others. Our awareness, sensitivity, open-mindedness, and flexibility are the primary governing factors that will guide us.

If we can accept the reality that other countries are likely to have a different culture than our own, without judgment, we are well on our way to living and working in a diverse environment. If we have difficulty doing so, we will be challenged and our effectiveness limited.

5) Given the pervasive impact of our perceptions, our ability to discover and adapt to those new realities requires us to be more aware of our perceptions and more agile in how we view them.

In many cases, while our beliefs seem natural and appropriate to us, they can be perceived as narrow-minded, or even ignorant to others. They can be biases that we didn't know we had. While they can be invisible to us, they are generally very evident to those around us.

Without conscious thought or awareness, our perceptions operate on automatic pilot. That which has been instilled in us by our native culture can yield awkward or even undesirable results in other settings.

6) The E.P.I.C. approach to gaining that awareness, along with its companion PPI instrument, is a starting point in gaining that awareness.

Having an increased awareness of what we believe and how those views were shaped is the first step, and is the objective of both the E.P.I.C. approach and its companion assessment, the Perception Power Index (PPI).

Those are provided as a means to take that first step. Ultimately, whatever mechanisms or instruments are used, having an increased understanding of your perceptions, their origins, and ways to better guide them are essential in today's workplace.

7) Ultimately, organizations must embrace and instill within its culture an increased awareness of the views and perceptions of its workforce.

Individual awareness alone is but a partial solution. One individual, working within an organizational culture of narrow-mindedness and ethnocentrism, has minimal impact on the interactions between individuals, both within and outside that organization.

Companies embrace and take actions to ensure that employees comply with company rules and policies. Likewise, they should take similar actions to ensure they establish a corporate culture that embraces global and multi-cultural attitudes. That begins with a dedicated campaign to address the potential cultural differences and biases inherent in the perceptions of its workforce.

* * * *

As we bring our treatise to a close, we do so not from the vantage point of business leaders, entrepreneurs, or academicians, but from that most prolific and eloquent philosopher of the human condition, William Shakespeare.

What's in a smile, a touch, movement, thought, or action that causes each of us to perceive things in a certain way? Two individuals may look at the very same event differently depending on their upbringing, cultures, or beliefs.

Shakespeare's Juliet asks what's the significance of a rose if given a different name? If different individuals have a different sense of smell or give it a different meaning, is it a precious gift? Is it a token of love? Or, is it an apology?

Would a rose by any other name smell as sweet, she asks? Well, it all depends on your perception!

References

Introduction

Friedman, Thomas L. (2005, April 3). "It's a Flat World After All." *The New York Times Magazine*. Accessed August 11, 2020 at https://www.nytimes.com/2005/04/03/magazine/its-a-flat-world-after-all.html

Krochow, Eva M., Ph. D. (2018, September 27). "How Many Decisions do we make each Day?" *Psychology Today*. Accessed August 11, 2020 at https://www.psychologytoday.com/us/blog/stretching-theory/201809/how-many-decisions-do-we-make-each-day

Seth, Aril. (2017, April). "Your Brain Hallucinates Your Conscious Reality," TED.com. Accessed August 11, 2020 at https://www.ted.com/talks/anil_seth_how_your_brain_hallucinates_your_conscious_reality?language=en

Chapter 1

Baack, D.W., Dow, D., Parente, R., & Bacon, D.R. (2015) "Confirmation Bias In Individual-Level Perceptions Of Psychic Distance: An Experimental Investigation." *Journal of International Business Studies*, 46 (8), 938-959. .

Brislin, Richard and Yoshida, Tomoko, eds. (1994). *Improving Intercultural Interactions: Modules for Cross-Cultural Training Programs*. Sage Publications, Thousand Oaks, CA.

Earley, P. Christopher, Soon, Ang and Tan, Joo-Seng. (2006). *CQ: Developing Cultural Intelligence.* Stanford, CA: Stanford Business Books.

Hamilton, Dr. Diane, (n.d.) "Continuous Learning Creates A Success Mindset with Naveen Jain." *Dr. Diane Hamilton Radio Show.* https://drdianehamilton.com/continuous-learning-creates-a-success-mindset-with-mike-federle-and-naveen-jain/ (accessed June 16, 2020).

Hamilton, Dr. Diane. (n.d.) "The Top 10 Most-Asked Questions Regarding the Curiosity Code Index." *Dr. Diane Hamilton Radio Show.* https://drdianehamilton.com/the-top-10-most-asked-questions-regarding-the-curiosity-code-index/ (accessed June 16, 2020).

Intersectoral Platform for a Culture of Peace and Non-Violence, Bureau for Strategic Planning, Eds. (2013). *Intercultural Competencies, Conceptual and Operational Framework.* UNESCO,. https://www.gvsu.edu/cms4/

asset/7D7DCFF8-C4AD-66A3-6344C7E690C4BFD9/
unesco-intercultural-competences-doc.pdf (accessed
June 16, 2020).

Livermore, David. (2015) *Leading With Cultural Intelligence,
The Real Secret to Success, Second Edition.* AMACOM.
https://culturalq.com/wp-content/uploads/2016/06/
Chapter_1_Leading_with_CQ_Livermore.pdf
(accessed June 16, 2020).

Lurie, Joe. (2015). *Perception and Deception: A Mind-Opening
Journey Across Culture.* Cultural Detective, Leawood,
KS.

Mercer, Julianna. (2015, January 25). "Understanding Your
Own Ethnocentrism," Penn State University OLEAD
410 blog. https://sites.psu.edu/global/2015/01/25/
understanding-your-own-ethnocentrism/ (accessed
June 16, 2020).

Mitchell, Robert. (2014, November 3). "Cultural Intelligence:
Everybody Needs It," *The Harvard Gazette.* https://
news.harvard.edu/gazette/story/2014/11/cultural-
intelligence-everybody-needs-it/ (accessed September
23, 2020).

Chapter 2

Covey, Stephen R. (2020). *The Seven Habits of Highly Effective
People.* Simon & Schuster, New York.

Foster, Richard J. (2018). *Celebration of Discipline: The*

Path to Spiritual Growth. 40th Anniversary Edition. HarperCollins, San Francisco.

Jackson, Ronald, editor. (2002). *Encyclopedia of Identity.* Sage Publications.

Krishnananda, Swami. (n.d.). *The Path to Freedom: Mastering the Art of Total Perception.* The Divine Life Society. https://www.swami-krishnananda.org/freedom/The.Path.to.Freedom.pdf (accessed online June 18, 2020).

Krishnamurthy, Pilani. (2002). *Science and Spirituality: A Vedanta Perception.* Bhavan's Book University.

Neyman, Roger Paul. (n.d.).*Fostering Hope: Harmonizing Science, Religion and the Arts.*

Chapter 3

Abramov, I., Gordon, J., Feldman, O. et al. (2012). Sex & vision I: Spatio-temporal resolution. *Biol Sex Differ* **3,** 20. https://doi.org/10.1186/2042-6410-3-20

Baron-Cohen, Simon. (2003). *The Essential Difference: Men, Women and the Extreme Male Brain.* Allen Lane.

Brizendine, Louanne. (2006). *The Female Brain.* Harmony Books, New York.

Brizendine, Louanne. (2010). *The Male Brain.* Harmony Books, New York.

Grant, Bob. (2013, December 4). "Male and Female Brains Wired Differently," *The Scientist.* https://www.the-scientist.com/the-nutshell/male-and-female-brains-wired-differently-38304 (accessed June 18, 2020).

Krivkovich, Alexis, Nadeau, Marie-Claude, et al. (2018, October 23). "Women in the Workplace 2018." *McKinsey and Company.* https://www.mckinsey.com/featured-insights/gender-equality/women-in-the-workplace-2018# (accessed June 22, 2020).

Litwin, Anne and Hahn, Sophie. (1995). *Managing in the Age of Change: Essential Skills to Manage Today's Workforce.* Burr Ridge, Illinois: IRWIN Professional Publishing.

Sprenger, Marilee. (1999). *Learning and Memory: The Brain in Action.* Association for Supervision and Curriculum Development, Alexandria, VA.

Chapter 4

Brown, Richard E. (2016, December 15). "Hebb and Cattell: The Genesis of the Theory of Fluid and Crystallized Intelligence." *Frontiers in human neuroscience* vol. 10 606. doi:10.3389/fnhum.2016.00606

Cherry, Kendra. (2019, July 17). "Gardner's Theory of Multiple Intelligences," *VeryWellmind.* https://www.verywellmind.com/gardners-theory-of-multiple-intelligences-2795161 (accessed June 23, 2020).

"Multiple Intelligences: What Does the Research Say?"

Edutopia, (March 8, 2013; updated July 20, 2016). https://www.edutopia.org/multiple-intelligences-research (accessed June 23, 2020).

Wachler, Brian Boxer. (2017). *Perceptual Intelligence: The Brain's Secret to Seeing Past Illusion, Misperception, and Self-Deception.* New World Library, Novato, CA.

Chapter 5

Christensen, J. F., Flexas, A., Calabrese, M., Gut, N. K., & Gomila, A. (2014). Moral judgment reloaded: a moral dilemma validation study. *Frontiers in psychology,* 5, 607. https://www.ncbi.nlm.nih.gov/pmc/articles/PMC4077230/ (accessed June 23, 2020).

Engelmann, Jan & Pogosyan, Marianna. (2013). "Emotion perception across cultures: The role of cognitive mechanisms." *Frontiers in psychology.* 4. 118. 10.3389/fpsyg.2013.00118.

Hamilton, Diane. (n.d.). "The Universality of Emotional Expressions with Dr. Paul Ekman,"*Dr. Diane Hamilton Radio Show.* Not dated. https://drdianehamilton.com/the-universality-of-emotional-expressions-with-dr-paul-ekman/ (accessed June 24, 2020).

Hamilton, Diane. (n.d.). "The Force of Curiosity with Francesca Gino and The Perception of Happiness with Silvia Garcia." *Dr. Diane Hamilton Radio Show.* https://drdianehamilton.com/the-force-of-curiosity-with-francesca-gino-and-the-perception-of-happiness-with-silvia-garcia/ (accessed June 23, 2020).

Pappas, Stephanie. (2014, January 24). "Love Makes Things Taste Sweeter," *Scientific American.* https://www.scientificamerican.com/article/love-makes-things-taste-sweeter/ (accessed June 23, 2020).

Pogosyan, Marianne, Ph.D. (2016, October 9). "Emotion Perception Across Cultures." *Psychology Today.* https://www.psychologytoday.com/us/blog/between-cultures/201610/emotion-perception-across-cultures (accessed June 23, 2020).

Ren, Dongning & Tan, Kenneth & Arriaga, Ximena & Chan, Kai. (2014) Sweet love. *Journal of Social and Personal Relationships.* 10.1177/0265407514554512.

Salovey, Peter, and John D. Mayer. (1990, March). "Emotional Intelligence." *Imagination, Cognition and Personality* 9, no. 3 : 185–211. doi:10.2190/DUGG-P24E-52WK-6CDG.

Susskind, Joshua & Lee, Daniel & Cusi, Andrée & Feiman, Roman & Grabski, Wojtek & Anderson, Adam. (2008) Expressing fear enhances sensory acquisition. *Nature Neuroscience.* 11. 843-50. 10.1038/nn.2138.

University of Cambridge. (2014, February). "Feeling powerless increases the weight of the world ... literally." *ScienceDaily.* www.sciencedaily.com/releases/2014/02/140203191735.htm. Accessed June 19, 2020.

Chapter 6

Aarons, J. E. (2012). *Fear of Failure*. R.R. Bowker.

Duhigg, C. (2016, February 25). What Google Learned From Its Quest to Build the Perfect Team. Retrieved September 26, 2020, from https://www.nytimes.com/2016/02/28/magazine/what-google-learned-from-its-quest-to-build-the-perfect-team.html

Maxwell, J. C. (2000). *Failing Forward: How To Make The Most Of Your Mistakes*. Thomas Nelson.

Tsaousides, T. (2015). *Brainblocks: Overcoming the 7 hidden barriers to success*. NY, NY: Prentice Hall Press.

Chapter 7

Lewis, C. (2005). A quote from The Magician's Nephew. Retrieved September 26, 2020, from https://www.goodreads.com/quotes/29188-what-you-see-and-what-you-hear-depends-a-great

Plato. (2008, August 27). The Republic (947753620 739535739 B. Jowett, Trans.). Retrieved September 26, 2020, from https://www.gutenberg.org/files/1497/1497-h/1497-h.htm

Poe, E. (n.d.). A Dream Within a Dream by Edgar Allan Poe. Retrieved September 26, 2020, from https://www.poetryfoundation.org/poems/52829/a-dream-within-a-dream

Chapter 8

Dhawan, E., & Joni, S. (2015). *Get big things done the power of connectional intelligence.* New York, NY: Palgrave Macmillan.

Edmondson, A. (2017, October). How to turn a group of strangers into a team. Retrieved September 26, 2020, from https://www.ted.com/talks/amy_edmondson_how_to_turn_a_group_of_strangers_into_a_team

Keijzer, P. (n.d.). Engage Consulting. Retrieved September 26, 2020, from http://paulkeijzer.com/engageco/

Kruse, K. (2019, October 25). PODCAST #307: Get Big Things Done: Erica Dhawan. Retrieved September 26, 2020, from https://leadx.org/articles/307-dhawan/

Meyer, E. (2014). *The culture map: Breaking through the invisible boundaries of global business.* New York: PublicAffairs.

Nevins, M., Dunlap, B., Pearce, N., & Robert B. Kaiser, T. (2019, January 15). How to Collaborate with People You Don't Like. Retrieved September 26, 2020, from https://hbr.org/2018/12/how-to-collaborate-with-people-you-dont-like

Steve Jobs. (n.d.). Retrieved September 26, 2020, from https://www.quotes.net/movies/steve_jobs_142224

Chapter 9

Cheung, B. (2013, February 19). How Innovation Happens (And Why It Doesn't, When It Doesn't). Retrieved September 26, 2020, from http://allthingsd.com/20130219/how-innovation-happens-and-why-it-doesnt-when-it-doesnt/

Griffith, T. L., & Sawyer, J. E. (2008, November/December). Changing Perceptions--And Triggering Innovation. Retrieved September 26, 2020, from https://iveybusinessjournal.com/publication/changing-perceptions-and-triggering-innovation/

James J. Gibson. (2020, September 13). Retrieved September 26, 2020, from https://en.wikipedia.org/wiki/James_J._Gibson

Naiman, L. (2014, June 6). Can Creativity be Taught? Here's What the Research Says. Retrieved September 26, 2020, from https://www.creativityatwork.com/2012/03/23/can-creativity-be-taught/

Projects, C. (2019, March 02). Quotes from the movie *Dead Poet's Society*. Retrieved September 26, 2020, from https://en.wikiquote.org/wiki/Dead_Poets_Society

Robinson, S. (2006, February). Do schools kill creativity? Retrieved September 26, 2020, from https://www.ted.com/talks/sir_ken_robinson_do_schools_kill_creativity

Roger Barker. (2020, September 13). Retrieved September 26, 2020, from https://en.wikipedia.org/wiki/Roger_Barker

Chapter 10

The Advancement of Learning. (2020, August 28). Retrieved September 26, 2020, from https://en.wikipedia.org/wiki/The_Advancement_of_Learning

Interview With Dave Gambrill, Digital Marketing Guru and Business Coach. (2019, May 03). Retrieved September 26, 2020, from https://herostory.org/dave-gambrill/

Kahneman, D. (2015). *Thinking, fast and slow*. New York: Farrar, Straus and Giroux.

Kallet, M. (2014). *Think smarter: Critical thinking to improve problem-solving and decision-making skills*. Hoboken, NJ: Wiley.

Konnikova, M. (2014). *Mastermind: How to think like Sherlock Holmes*. Edinburgh: Canongate.

Lawrence, J., & Chester, L. (2014). *Engage the fox: A business fable about thinking critically and motivating your team*. Austin, TX: Greenleaf Book Group Press.

Meltzer, D. C. (2019). *Game-time decision making: High-scoring business strategies from the biggest names in sports*. New York: McGraw-Hill.

Siebold, S. (2010). *177 Mental Toughness Secrets of the World Class*. London House Press.

Chapter 11

Alan Wilson Quotes. (n.d.). Retrieved September 26, 2020, from https://www.brainyquote.com/authors/alan-wilson-quotes

Berger, W. (2019). *A more beautiful question: The power of inquiry to spark breakthrough ideas.* Vancouver, B.C.: Langara College.

Berger, W. (2020). Why Curious People Are Destined for the C-Suite. Retrieved September 26, 2020, from https://hbrascend.org/topics/why-curious-people-are-destined-for-the-c-suite/

Cashman, K. (2017). *Leadership from the inside out: Becoming a leader for life.* Oakland, CA: BK Berrett-Koehler.

Confino, J. (2012, April 24). Unilever's Paul Polman: Challenging the corporate status quo. Retrieved September 26, 2020, from https://www.theguardian.com/sustainable-business/paul-polman-unilever-sustainable-living-plan

Cribbin, S. (2012, August 06). Information Gap Theory. Retrieved September 26, 2020, from https://siobhancribbin.wordpress.com/2012/08/06/information-gap-theory-10/

Dave Ulrich. (2020, June 08). Retrieved September 26, 2020, from https://en.wikipedia.org/wiki/Dave_Ulrich

Dr Diane Hamilton Interviews Dr Francesca Gino [Video file].

(2019, February 26). Retrieved September 26, 2020, from https://www.youtube.com/watch?v=WoEnfnD253M

Garcia, S. (n.d.). Happiest Places to Work. Retrieved September 26, 2020, from https://www.happiestplacestowork.org/

Gino, F. (2020). *Rebel Talent: Why it pays to break the rules at work and in life*. NY, NY: William Morrow.

Grazer, B., & Fishman, C. (2016). *A curious mind: The secret to a bigger life*. New York: Simon & Schuster Paperbacks.

Hamilton, D. (2018). *Cracking the curiosity code: The key to unlocking human potential*. Columbus, OH: Gatekeeper Press.

Hartung, F., & Renner, B. (2011). [PDF] Social Curiosity and Interpersonal Perception: A Judge × Trait Interaction: Semantic Scholar. Retrieved September 26, 2020, from https://www.semanticscholar.org/paper/Social-Curiosity-and-Interpersonal-Perception%3A-A-%C3%97-Hartung-Renner/72859844c92b85fef4460a3562d36ebcc464ce53

Jeffrey H. Dyer. (2019, March 18). The Innovator's DNA. Retrieved September 26, 2020, from https://hbr.org/2009/12/the-innovators-dna

Jeffrey R. Immelt Quotes. (n.d.). Retrieved September 26, 2020, from https://www.brainyquote.com/authors/jeffrey-r-immelt-quotes

Maxwell, J. C. (2000). *Failing Forward: How To Make The Most Of Your Mistakes*. Thomas Nelson.

Porter, T. (2015). *Intellectual Humility, Mindset, and Learning*. Stanford University.

Chapter 12

Ackerman, Joshua & Nocera, Christopher & Bargh, John. (2010). Incidental Haptic Sensations Influence Social Judgments and Decisions. Science (New York, N.Y.). 328. 1712-5. 10.1126/science.1189993.

Farber, N. (2016, September 18). The Truth About the Law of Attraction. *Psychology Today.* Retrieved September 26, 2020, from https://www.psychologytoday.com/us/blog/the-blame-game/201609/the-truth-about-the-law-attraction

Juma, A. (2015, December 22). The 6 Principles of Influence: How To Master Persuasion. Retrieved September 26, 2020, from https://medium.com/@alyjuma/the-6-principles-of-influence-how-to-master-persuasion-2f8c581da38b

Laing, R. (1970). Knots. Retrieved September 26, 2020, from https://qdoc.tips/knots-ronald-laing-1970pdf-3-pdf-free.html

Mudallal, Z. (2014, December 31). How psychologists used a mobile game to make airport baggage screening better.

Quartz. Retrieved September 26, 2020, from https://qz.com/318732/how-psychologists-used-a-mobile-game-to-make-airport-baggage-screening-better/

A quote from The Book of Secrets. (n.d.). Retrieved September 26, 2020, from https://www.goodreads.com/quotes/497783-if-you-obsess-over-whether-you-are-making-the-right

Schwartz, B. (2005, July). The paradox of choice. Retrieved September 26, 2020, from https://www.ted.com/talks/barry_schwartz_the_paradox_of_choice

USS Pueblo (AGER-2). (2020, September 24). Retrieved September 26, 2020, from https://en.wikipedia.org/wiki/USS_Pueblo_(AGER-2)

Chapter 13

7 Simon Sinek quotes that will change your thinking on leadership and business. (2010). Retrieved September 26, 2020, from https://www.businesscentral.net/7-simon-sinek-quotes-that-will-change-your-thinking-on-leadership-and-business

Buckingham, M., & Coffman, C. (2016). *First, break all the rules: What the world's greatest managers do differently.* Washington, D.C.: Gallup Press.

Kruse, K. (2015, June 26). What Is Employee Engagement. *Forbes.com* Retrieved September 26, 2020, from https://

www.forbes.com/sites/kevinkruse/2012/06/22/employee-engagement-what-and-why/

Lee, D. (n.d.). Human Nature At Work: Helping Leaders Inspire the Best in People. Retrieved September 26, 2020, from https://humannatureatwork.com/

Nelson, B. (2005). *1001 ways to reward employees*. Workman Publishing.

Nelson, B., & Economy, P. (2005). *The Management Bible*. Hoboken, NJ: John Wiley & Sons.

Reichheld, F. F., & Teal, T. (2008). *The loyalty effect: The hidden force behind growth, profits, and lasting value*. Boston, Mass: Harvard Business School Press.

Sheridan, K. (2012). *Building a magnetic culture: How to attract and retain top talent to create an engaged, productive workforce*. McGraw-Hill.

Voltaire Quotes. (n.d.). Retrieved September 26, 2020, from https://www.brainyquote.com/quotes/voltaire_109642

Chapter 14

9 Crucial Traits that New Managers Should Develop. (2019, September 17). Retrieved September 26, 2020, from https://www.notredameonline.com/resources/leadership-and-management/9-crucial-traits-that-new-managers-should-develop/

Clegg, C. (2019, August 5). Achieving Lifetime Employability. Retrieved September 26, 2020, from https://www.powerfluence.com/post/achieving-lifetime-employability

Daskal, L. (2018, June 21). Leadership Takes Wonder to be Successful - Lolly Daskal: Leadership. Retrieved September 26, 2020, from https://www.lollydaskal.com/leadership/leadership-of-wonder/

Goldstein, J. (2016, September 15). Leadership Assessment. Retrieved September 26, 2020, from https://joelgoldstein.com/leadership-assessment/

How Skybell founder defeated his counter mind. (2018, June 29). Retrieved September 26, 2020, from https://mixergy.com/interviews/skybell-with-andrew-thomas/

Hyatt, M., & Harkavy, D. (2016). *Living forward: A proven plan to stop drifting and get the life you want*. Grand Rapids, MI: Baker Books, Baker Publishing Group.

Quoteresearch. (2018, October 05). If Your Actions Inspire Others To Dream More, Learn More, Do More and Become More, You Are a Leader. Retrieved September 26, 2020, from https://quoteinvestigator.com/2011/07/03/inspire-dream-leader/

Spence, J. (2011). *Awesomely Simple: Essential business strategies for turning ideas into action*. ReadHowYouWant.com.

Spence, J. (2019, February). The Leader of the Future. Retrieved September 26, 2020, from https://www.ted.

com/talks/john_spence_the_leader_of_the_future

Chapter 15

Stephen Covey Quotes. (n.d.). Retrieved September 26, 2020, from https://www.brainyquote.com/quotes/stephen_covey_138246

Chapter 16

Hamilton, D. (2018). *Cracking the curiosity code: The key to unlocking human potential.* Columbus, OH: Gatekeeper Press.

A quote from The Knight. (n.d.). Retrieved September 26, 2020, from https://www.goodreads.com/quotes/519224-follow-the-evidence-to-where-it-leads-even-if-the

TOP 22 QUOTES BY ROBERT A. BURTON: A-Z Quotes. (n.d.). Retrieved September 26, 2020, from https://www.azquotes.com/author/38420-Robert_A_Burton

CPSIA information can be obtained
at www.ICGtesting.com
Printed in the USA
LVHW111705300621
691558LV00018B/37